Encouraging Thoughts

Doug Creamer

Encouraging Thoughts

Doug Creamer

Copyright © 2000, 2016

Cover design by Robin E. Buchanan

Illustrations by Bridgett A. McBride

Photo of author by Andrew McCarn & Sydney Byerly

Published by Faith Farm Publishing Company

P.O. Box 777

Faith, North Carolina 28041

Scripture taken from the HOLY BIBLE, NEW INTERNATIONAL VERSION. Copyright 1973, 1978, 1984 International Bible Society. Used by permission of Zondervan Bible Publishers.

Some of the material in this book is based on material that has appeared elsewhere in another form.

ISBN: 0-9743935-4-1
ISBN-13: 978-0-9743935-4-4

Published and printed in the United States of America

DEDICATION

I dedicate this book to the Lord Jesus Christ. He is the source of my inspiration. Writing has always been the weakest part of my life. That is why I delight in II Corinthians 12:9 & 10.

But he said to me, "My grace is sufficient for you, for my power is made perfect in weakness." Therefore I will boast all the more gladly about my weaknesses, so that Christ's power may rest on me. That is why, for Christ's sake, I delight in weaknesses, in insults, in hardships, in persecutions, in difficulties. For when I am weak, then I am strong.

I would also like to dedicate this book to my wife, Marissa. She has listened to and encouraged me in my hopes and dreams. She has also given me the time I needed to complete this book. She is a true gift from God. Marissa, thank you for your help and thank you for being a part of my life.

Table of Contents

Holidays

3 Cute + 3 Special = 6 worth reading 165

SPECIAL THANKS

First and foremost, thanks to Marissa, my wife. She has been a constant source of encouragement. She gave me the freedom and time I needed to write this book. Then she took time to read most of the book and offer suggestions on how to improve my writing. Marissa constantly challenges me to pursue excellence in my writing. For her love, dedication, and support I am forever in her debt.

I am thankful that Bridgett McBride willingly drew the illustrations for my book. They are perfect!

I am extremely grateful to the following group of people who gave of their time freely to help proof read my manuscript: Doug and Emily Moose, Linda Huneycutt, Boyd Nash, Denise Ritner, and my lovely wife, Marissa Creamer. This team of people helped to edit my book so you the reader would be glad you bought it. Thank you one and all.

I am also thankful to Mark at Press Printers in Albemarle, NC who helped guide me through the printing process.

There are a host of people like my grandmother who have encouraged me throughout this project. To each of you I express a heart-felt thanks. If you hadn't been there when I needed a little boost, this project would never have been completed.

To my many readers, thank-you for your support. I hope you enjoy this book and that it will be a source of encouragement to you. God bless you and may His peace surround you.

(Additional note for this revised edition.)

When I decided that I wanted to put Encouraging Thoughts on Amazon with my other books, I did not realize what I had to do. I had all the files from the book, but nothing could open those old files. The only way I could get this book in electronic form was to re-type it. That's when I decided to contact a former student and ask for some help. Maggie Hill re-typed the entire book into Word so I could upload it…a huge thank you to Maggie. Then I needed help with the cover of the book and Robin Buchanan stopped by my classroom one day. She is also a former student who has a degree in graphic design. She was more than excited to give me a hand with this updated book. What an awesome job she did too! Thank you both for helping me make this book available on Amazon. Bless you both!

Influences

Many, if not all, authors have what is called a dedication page for their book. On it they thank the people who helps to bring the book to market. There are usually editors, publishers and family members included in the list. Well, I would like to approach it from a different angle. I would like to mention specific people who have impacted my life and encouraged me to write.

I hope you will read this and not skip to the next article. The reason I ask you to read is that you may never know how you have "influenced" others in the path of their life. I hope as you read this you will discover the importance of words of encouragement and the power they have on others' lives.

One more thing before I begin. I make it a point to never mention a person's name in my columns. I do this to protect the people who are the subjects of my column and to help you, as my reader, to identify with my writing. My family falls under a different category, but since most of you do not know them personally, I feel comfortable. I also avoid names so people won't perform around me just to get into my column. Today, and in this one instance, I am breaking that rule. Look out world, here we come!

For those of you who read my very first column, you may remember that I wrote how John Boy Walton was my first writing hero. Here was a young man who wrote and he was respected for his talent. I loved watching the family and seeing all the love and concern for one another. Most of all I loved how John Boy wrote and the power he had with words. I liked seeing him get his first printing press and the joy he had as he pulled the first paper off his press. I remember how bad I felt for him when their house burnt down. John Boy had a manuscript burn up in that fire.

Many evenings after the Walton's went off I would go to my room and write about some of the events that occurred in my family. I know the writing wasn't really worth the paper it was written on, but for me it showed my heart's desire to write. If I had an early influence in my life, it would definitely be John Boy Walton.

Another influence in my writing life would be my mother. My

mother always made me feel great about whatever I wanted to do when I grew up. However, I am sure she probably laughed her head off after I told her I wanted to be a writer. The reason I feel my mother probably laughed her head off after I told her I wanted to be a writer is that when I was a kid I was a terrible writer. The worst! AWFUL! PU! You get the picture. She never let me know how she truly felt, she always encouraged whatever desire I was currently expressing.

When I was in Junior and Senior High School and I had a paper due for some class, I would always show it to my mother. I use to think that was always a big mistake because she would always find tons of errors. I hated it. Oops, sorry Mom, I don't HATE anything....I disliked it an awful lot! You know she was just trying to help me and spare my poor English teachers the sheer torture of having to read one of my papers. Mom, the truth is, I do appreciate all you did to help me be a better writer....NOW!

One year for Christmas or my birthday my mother gave me a completely empty book. I remember looking at her like she had lost her marbles. I knew I was a poor reader at the time too, but come on, an empty book was ridiculous. She told me it was a very special book that I was supposed to write. I don't ever remember getting such a special gift. My mother in her own way was encouraging me to be a writer.

I always felt sorry for my English teachers in high school. I was such a terrible writer with the worst handwriting. In the eleventh grade, I had Mrs. Pleasants as my English teacher. There was an incident in her room that crystalized my desire to write that goes something like this:

Mrs. Pleasants was introducing a unit on writing. I should point out that I sat in the back of her class. I was in the far left hand corner from her desk. I was also a very average "C" student in her class. Anyway, she stood in front of the class and asked us what a writer would look like. A student who sat in the front of the class raised her hand and once called upon pointed directly at me and said, "Him."

Mrs. Pleasants looked at me for a while and I am sure thought, "How could she have missed it so badly. I don't think I will ever ask that question again if they think he looks like a writer!" After the moment of horror, she recovered and asked the student "Why did you choose him?"

To which the student responded, "He's quiet. And you can tell he thinks about things a lot. I think he will be a writer."

Mrs. Pleasants looked at me again and asked, "Doug, what do you think about that?"

"I have done some writing and I hope she is right." and the truth is it did sound great to me. I always wondered how that girl knew I wanted to write. Poor Mrs. Pleasants tried to pick the pieces of her shredded lesson up and proceed on with class. Mrs. Pleasants was an excellent English teacher and so, with several glances in my direction, she started telling us about writers and authors.

The other high school teacher who influenced me to be a writer was my senior English teacher, Miss Christ. (Now married to my senior Government teacher, Mr. Piccello, a good story in itself.) She was a first-year teacher so she was young and very good looking. That made senior English class a pleasure to attend. One of the funniest things in my high school career happened the first day of school. I simply must tell this story (even though it doesn't relate).

Miss Christ was assigned lunch duty. So the first day of school, one of the hottest guys goes up and starts talking to this young, good looking teacher. The guy thought that she was a new student at our school. So before lunch was over he asked her out on a date. She had to tell him that she was a teacher. This guy asked the teacher out in front of some of his friends who quickly spread it through the whole school. He was really embarrassed. But it gets better. Right after lunch we all reported to fifth period. This guy had English right after lunch and guess who his teacher was? Boy, I bet he thought that was one long English class that day.

Anyway, back to how Miss Christ influenced me. Miss Christ came to Kempsville High School in Virginia Beach with some new ideas. She felt that seniors should keep journals. It was a free write activity. We were supposed to write for five minutes every day in our journal. We would turn them in and she would read them and give us some feedback. We were allowed to write about anything that interested us. It was in her English class that I wrote openly about my faith. She always wrote nice comments about what I wrote and she encouraged me to write more.

Before I graduated from high school I was already writing. I wrote short one-paragraph thoughts about God. I gave them away at a part-time job to any customer who would take one. It was during this time that I got the chance to meet Og Mandino. Og is an inspirational speaker and writer. I spent almost an hour at a book store talking to him between other people who came to get an autograph from his new book. He gave me his address and I wrote him a letter with lots of questions. He wrote a letter back that I have kept ever since. It was a real source of encouragement.

My father left his impression on me too. After I graduated from high school, I announced to my family that I was not going to college. I told them that I wanted to become a writer. That went over like a lead balloon.

Dad sat me down one evening to discuss the economics of my decision. He showed me the costs of living on my own, which I had planned to do, and explained how difficult it would be. He was very logical and even tempered about the whole thing. He told me I would be better off if I went to college and got an education. Besides he thought the experiences of college would improve my writing abilities.

He could tell he was beginning to get through. So that's when he told me I could be a writer after college and that if my writing didn't work out, I would always have my education to fall back on. He also said that if I wanted nice things, and I did, that college would probably be the key to them. So I reluctantly put the pen down and headed for college. At the time I wasn't exactly happy with the choice but now as I look back, it was excellent advice from my father. So Dad – Thanks – I appreciate it.

The next person to influence my writing career was Tom Watson (That's not the golfer Dad). I never met Tom Watson, I only talked to him by phone. He lived close to Asheboro, NC and was a good friend of an elder in my church. I use the past tense here because he has gone home to be with the Lord.

I called him one evening and we talked for about forty-five minutes. I told him I wanted to be a writer, mainly a novelist. Tom listened patiently to my dreams and then told me I needed some practical experience. He suggested that I start by trying to write a weekly column for a paper.

I thought about Tom's suggestion for a long time before I took action. Finally, I decided maybe he was right. I worked on several pieces and prepared to meet some editors. I talked to several editors who turned me down, but all encouraged me to continue my quest. Rejection is difficult to take after a while and I nearly gave up on Tom's suggestion. Finally, as hope was dwindling, I decided to give the Stanly News & Press (SNAP) a shot.

I knew Mike Eudy at the SNAP and I gave him a call. Mike gave me several excellent pointers before I met with Kate Dickson, the editor of the SNAP. Kate read my material and decided to give me a try. She decided that I would only appear occasionally and there would be no pay. I had my first chance and I took it. Thanks Mike and Kate, I appreciate it,

When my first article was published I am not sure who was more excited me or my brother. My brother Dennis works at the Greensboro News and Record. When I told him I was published, he almost came through the phone he was so excited. In the beginning, each time I was published he was very excited for me. For Christmas that year he got a copy of my first article and had the whole page printed on paper that will not fade. Then he got it framed. I keep that hanging in my office. What a wonderful treasure.

There is a local couple who have been very encouraging to me as a writer and they are Doug & Emily Moose. Emily is the first person that I know that hung one of my columns up in her office cubical. Now that's encouraging! Doug teaches beside me at North Stanly and he has been a constant source of encouragement. Many times he has called my attention to topics that needed addressing. He has also been writing a book and has allowed me the privilege to encourage him in his writing.

There are a host of others who encourage me as I write to encourage you, I wish I could devote a paragraph to each person and because I do not does not diminish my gratitude for their help and encouragement in my writing career. Here it goes:
*My grandmother who challenges me to grow deeper spiritually and to discover the things that are really important in life.

*My sister Denise who tries to get herself or her children into my columns. I appreciate her encouragement and her excitement and interest in the things I have written.
*My sister Deb who encourages me each time she sees me.
*Nancy Smoak, Linda Huneycutt, Terry Leitch and Boyd Nash who encourage and challenge me at work.
*Doug Louie who encouraged me to diversify.
*That special couple who took me out for some ice cream.
*Staci Burris & Breanne Burris are two faithful readers who challenged me to write better last year. They read my columns and told me what they thought. Thanks ladies.
*Liz Nichols for her gift of encouragement.
There are many others I could mention and probably should mention but space will not allow me to do it. The Lord knows who you are and I pray that your reward will be great in heaven. Again to all those who encourage me to encourage you I couldn't write if it weren't for your encouraging words.
Thank you and God Bless.

READ THIS

Why did I write a section about "Influences" in my life? It's simple. You never know the influence you are having on others and how that will impact their lives. So I encourage you to be one of those people who spends some time each day encouraging others. You never know where that person may go and whose lives they may be able to touch because of your encouraging word.

I encourage you to be an encourager of others!

The Beach

I have always loved going to the beach. It seems to be the one place that I can quiet myself and listen to my Heavenly Father. We all need to find that place where we can hear the voice of the Lord to direct our feet in life. Now you know I am not about hearing God audibly. I mean sensing in your spirit what God would have you to do. The beach is that kind of place for me.

The beach is so peaceful it allows me to think and be creative. All the distractions of everyday life seem to stay home and I can be about the business of relaxing. I enjoy reading a good book and writing inspirational thoughts.

Our favorite thing to do is walk the beach. I can walk for miles and hardly ever feel tired. I like the water lapping up on my feet. I like watching the shore birds run up and down the beach after their prey. The smell of the salt air does something good to your insides. You see it all works together to create an awesome effect.

As you read or re-read the following columns from the beach allow your Father to touch your spirit. I hope and pray that you will be refreshed just as I was when I wrote them. Even now as I reflect on the messages contained in them I am touched once again by the wonderful word of the Father. Set your spirit free to be touched by these words.

Most of all I encourage you to find that place in your life where you can meet with your Heavenly Father. For you it may be on a boat, in a plane, on a hiking trail, in your garden or even on your back porch. Find that place and meet with your Father often. I sense that our Heavenly Father wants to meet with each of us in that quiet place.

God's Love

I recently went to the beach for a vacation. I love the beach because it is a peaceful place that allows for times of reflection. I walk the beach and think about life's problems and try to figure out some answers. When I was down there this time I was thinking about God's love and how people view His love very differently. Some feel God created everything and then left the scene for us to work it out. Others, myself included, feel God is very much involved in our daily lives and concerned about our problems. The third group feels it is somewhere between the two.

As I was walking down the beach, I remembered one passage of scripture that says, "How precious to me are your thoughts, O God! How vast is the sum of them! Were I to count them, they would outnumber the grains of sand." (Ps. 139:17 & 18) I got my hands wet then put them into dry sand so I could count the grains of sand. I know that over two hundred were on one finger alone. Then I looked down the hazy beach as far as the eye could see in both directions there was sand. Imagine that, if two hundred grains of sand fit on one hand, imagine how much God must be thinking about us.

I decided to read the rest of that Psalm. These are just a few of the thoughts from that Psalm: ".. you are familiar with all my ways. Before a word is on my tongue you know it completely," ".. you knit me together in my mother's womb." ".. your eyes saw my unformed body." There are plenty of other thoughts not only in this Psalm but throughout the whole Bible that express God's interest in every detail of our lives. This is why I find it difficult to believe that God isn't involved intimately in our lives.

There is a popular song that concerns me because it expresses a belief contrary to what the Bible teaches. The one line in the song that bothers me goes, "God is watching us, from a distance." That implies to me that God cannot and is not intimately involved in our daily lives. This is, however, what many people believe. They think that God has to deal with the big problems such as hunger, war, peace and world leaders. They believe that God put us here and gave us the where-with-all to solve our own problems and that we should not "bug" God with them.

What these people fail to understand is one of God's character qualities. God is omnipresent. No other created thing including the devil can be omnipresent. So what is omnipresent? That is the quality of being everywhere at the same time. So that means I might feel the presence of God very strongly at one moment and someone over in China may feel God's presence in the same way at exactly the same time. If God can be omnipresent, then He can be concerned about big world problems. AND He can be concerned about the little problems that I face.

It sure is comforting to me to know that God thinks about me like the grains of sand on the beach. After a trip to the beach you always tend to bring some sand home, no matter how hard you try to leave it there. The next time I go to the beach I won't get upset at the sand I bring home, I'll just think of it as God's thoughts coming home with me.

How precious to me are your thoughts, O God!
How vast is the sum of them.
Were I to count them they would outnumber
the grains of sand.
Psalm 139:17 & 18

The Places We Meet God

I just came in from a long walk back and forth across my yard. That's right, I just cut the grass. Cutting the grass is one kind of exercise that I try to maintain in my life, in other words I don't own a riding mower. Anyway, this morning's walk was a hot and sweaty one.

I have enjoyed beautiful walks the last three mornings. You guessed it, I've been to the beach again. I must confess that even though I got hot and sweaty during those walks on the beach, I enjoyed them very much. The roar of the lawn mower does not compare to the roar of the ocean. I tell you what, I missed the ocean this morning.

What is it about the beach and the ocean that seem to affect us? I finished up work one day and we headed to the beach the next. I was still feeling stressed out from a long year of dealing with students and adults. I thought that as I drove to the beach the stress level would come down, but it didn't. I arrived at the beach tired and in need of a change.

There was a pleasant gentleman who helped us to our room and unloaded all out stuff. We put a few things away and then stepped onto our balcony. That's the moment it happened. We both could feel it. We sat down on the balcony and within minutes every bit of stress was taken away by the wonderful soothing sound of the ocean. We both allowed every care to disappear, to evaporate in that peaceful place.

The next few days as I walked the beach I tried to figure out why this happens. I know I am not the only one who gets such mental release at the beach. I have a friend who tells me that when he and his wife cross the bridge that leads to their place, they feel the same thing. What is it about the beach that has the power to take all that stress out of our lives?

My first thought is that most of us leave our problems at home. Everybody has problems in their life. Sometimes our problems are small and seem manageable, other times they seem larger than life itself. When we are away from our homes, where our problems live, we can forget about them. One of the things I like about the beach is that I find I can sort through my problems. I always feel better about facing them when I get home.

The beach is also a place where life doesn't feel so demanding. I imagine if you have children that may not be the case. When we are at the beach there is no grass to cut, dishes to wash, things that need repair and gardens that need weeding. I can do different things like walk the beach, read a good book, swim in the pool or the ocean, take a nap in the afternoon, write or even watch a good movie. Life's pace seems to be slower at the beach, a much needed change.

I also find the beach to be a place of solitude. As I walk the beach I talk to God about my problems. Because my spirit is much more quiet and I am less distracted, I feel the Lord's presence. I also feel him showing me the answers to life's problems. The amazing thing is that the problems seem so much smaller at the beach. How can any problem seem difficult when the God of the whole universe is standing right beside you to help you through it?

When I am at the beach I feel the Lord's presence and His all-encompassing love. Although my home is supposed to be a refuge from the world, sometimes the world finds a way to sneak in. At the beach it's different, I always feel peace. The world's cares seem miles away (actually they are waiting for me to get home!) God's love seems almost tangible when I am at the beach. While I am there I see the beauty, I feel the warm sunshine and the cool breeze and life's problems just seem to float away.

How can you feel transformed and ready to meet life's problems head on? You need to find that place for you where it's peaceful and quiet where you can hear the voice of the Lord. Good Luck and may God's peace be with you.

The World Yells, God Whispers

We went to the beach just after school let out. Believe me it was a much needed get away. We walked the beach, swam in the pool, did some reading, took some naps, thought about life and ate some great food.

The hotel where we stay is located one mile north of the Myrtle Beach strip. There are homes between our hotel and the hotels on the strip. This makes for a very peaceful place to walk the beach and think about my life and to pray. I am not much of an ocean swimmer any more but give me a quiet beach and I could walk for miles.

I always look forward to going to the beach mainly because that is one place my soul gets quiet enough to hear from the Lord. I think expecting to hear from the Lord plays an important part in that process. This particular trip I really needed to hear from the Lord. I was feeling burnt out and I needed a rekindling. I needed a touch from the Spirit to be rejuvenated.

The enemy was aware of this and he had plans to stop it. You see the beach has always been a place where I can visualize the battle between the kingdom of God and the kingdom of the enemy. On the one side you have the ocean signifying the power of God kept under control. The tides come in and go out but the water has a stopping place.

The land screams the cries of the world. "Come enjoy the pleasures of life! There are plenty things to do. We have something to meet every desire of your mind and flesh." It's sort of like the temptation of Christ when Satan shows Jesus all the kingdoms of this world. They certainly seem desirable and pleasurable. The world is calling you and I to come enjoy these pleasures that anyone can plainly see.

Then you look to the ocean and it is calling you to come and die to those pleasures and receive new life. You have to trust the Lord to raise you up again if you choose to die. So there you and I stand looking out at the pleasures of this life which we can plainly see. Then we look at the ocean and the life we cannot plainly see. We don't know where the Lord might lead us and we can't see what lies ahead.

We look back to the world and see the instant gratification it offers. What we fail to see is that those apparent pleasures are just fronts to a bunch of traps, jails, dead ends and death. We don't see or maybe we don't want to see that the world's pleasures lead to death. It's hopelessness. It's separation from our Heavenly Father.

This is one of those paradoxes. We can choose what appears to be the good life which is actually death. Or we can choose what we know is death but will ultimately lead to life. Christ made that decision when He went to the cross for us. He chose death so that we all might have life. That's what He means when He says take up your cross and follow me.

The enemy's call is like irresistible sirens but God's call is like a soft whisper. Do you remember when Elijah was on the mountain waiting for God? There was a mighty wind, an earthquake and a fire but God was not in them. Then there was a gentle whisper calling out to him. The Lord was in the whisper.

The Lord wants to meet with us and to talk to us. The problem is the world is so loud that we can't quite hear Him. We need to remove the distractions and find a quiet place where we can hear the breath and the very heart of God. Listen…I hear a gentle whisper calling…Listen!

The Lord was not in the powerful wind.
The Lord was not in the earthquake.
The Lord was not in the fire.
The Lord came to Elijah in a gentle
whisper.

I LOVE YOU

Last week I told you we went to the beach and that I hoped to hear from the Lord. I was hoping for some profound word that would rebuild my soul. One morning I headed out to the beach by myself for a long walk with the Lord. The beach was quiet and I felt like I had it all to myself. I said, "Lord here I am all alone waiting to hear from you. What's on your heart for me at this time?" The answer came like the soft breeze blowing on my face. "Son, I love you."

The second I heard the answer I began to argue with the Lord. "How can you love me? Don't you see the sin in my heart? Can't you see where I have rebelled and not been the obedient son you want me to be? Look at all my evil desires? You know me, you know how faithless I have been at times. How can you love me?" I continued to argue in my heart with the Lord even naming my sins one by one.

When I got back to the hotel my heart was still troubled because I still hadn't accepted the simple encouraging word. I decided the best thing I could do was go for another walk on the beach. I needed to wrestle with the Lord some more. This time I walked the beach where it was packed with people.

I felt like I was walking through the world with all its temptations. I walked briskly with eyes fixed on the beach in front of me. The world seemed to be closing in on me. I began to wonder if I had made a mistake choosing to walk in the crowded area of the beach. How could I hear from the Lord with all the distractions? Then slowly I emerged to a quiet place on the other side of all the people. It was there that I finally felt a spiritual release and my soul was at peace.

I listened again for the Lord and the word came like a whisper to my soul, "Son I love you!" The word penetrated the walls of my soul to the depths of my being. "I love you!" The how and the why melted away as my soul began to drink in the life those words provided.

Then the Lord allowed me to see something that helped to seal it in my soul. There was a father playing ball with his son on the beach. The young child had one of those really fat plastic bats and the father was pitching him one of those plastic balls. The father pitched the ball several times coaching the son but he still missed. The father persisted in trying to teach the son how to hit the ball. Finally, the son swung hard and got a line drive right into the father's bare, sunburnt chest. Thud! The father winced and took a deep breath. Then the father went over rubbed the son's head and gave him a hug, congratulating him on his hit.

I, on the other hand, laughed out loud. I think I laughed for five minutes about it and I am laughing even as I write these words. But I learned something from watching them. I learned that even though I do things that hurt my Father, he still loves me. If my heart is repentant before my Father, He will forgive me. He will also be there to let me know, "Son I love you!"

I think the word finally sank in. The word was simple but it brought life to a tired and needy soul. Maybe we expect God to always be deep and complex, when in reality He may be very simple. Take salvation for example, many people believe there is a list of things you must do before you can be saved. The truth, according to- Romans 10:9 & 10, is that if we confess with our lips Jesus is Lord and we believe in our hearts that God raised Him from the dead, we will be saved. It's that simple.

The Lord wants us all to hear from his heart. He desires to encourage all of us to seek Him and to know Him. Sometimes when we are tired and weary and we are hungry to hear from the Lord, the word of the Lord may come to us in a simple way. "My son (or My daughter), I love you!"

The Lord would say unto you,
"You are my child and I love you."

Eagles

Birds

Animals

Cats

Dogs

Goats

Contentment

Keep your lives free from the love of money
and be content with what you have.
Hebrews 13:5

For the past few months I have noticed a family of goats living in a pen by the side of the road. They have all that I think goats need; food, a good shelter, some trees for shade and a nice pond for water. However, the other day I noticed the goats stretching their necks through the fence eating the grass on the other side. The grass is always greener on the other side of the fence.

This put me to thinking about contentment. I am convinced those goats have all they need to survive without reaching through that fence to the grass on the other side. I wonder how many of us are like those goats? Are we content with the things we have or are we striving for more? Do we try to keep up with the Jones or are we content with what God has given us? When it comes to getting something new, can we take it or leave it? Do we think, as advertisers want us to think, "gotta have it!?"

Paul writes in Philippians that he has learned the secret of contentment. Why did he call it a secret? It must in some way be obtainable and it is certainly a desirable quality. The question remains, "How do I acquire the "secret" of the contentment?"

The starting place is easy to find. I know I came in to the world with nothing. My parents provided everything for me. Now I work to provide for my own wants and needs. I also know that when the end of my life arrives, I will not be able to take anything with me to the other side. So that implies that whatever God allows me to acquire while I am here will stay here. I do have to chuckle at the bumper sticker that says, "Whoever has the most toys at the end wins!"

But seriously, folks, with the basic idea that we can't take it with us, we should look to our Lord for his thoughts on owning things. It's hard to imagine that he came into the world just like we did, with nothing. If acquisition of assets is to be our goal then Jesus would have lived that way to be an example for us. Jesus was more concerned about people than he was things. In fact Jesus taught in the sermon on the mount that we should not be concerned about the material things in life. He taught that we should seek His kingdom and His righteousness and then trust that God would provide for all of our needs. (Please note, it says our needs, not wants; there is a big difference.)

Paul wrote to the young minister Timothy that he would be satisfied if he has food and clothing. How many of us would be content with food, clothing and a basic shelter to live in? I know I personally have been struggling with the desire for a new car. My car is getting older and it has over 150,000 miles. One of the things that I have to constantly remind myself lately is that the car is paid for and it runs pretty well. I have been trying to work on being thankful that I even own a car, especially since it does not break down. But those shiny new cars look so tempting.

There are two key things that we need to learn to understand the "secret" of contentment. The first is that we need to be thankful for the things that God had given us. If you look around your home as I have recently done at mine, you will discover many things for which you can be thankful. The second, and more difficult one, is that we have to remember that God has promised to meet all our needs. This means that we have to trust Him that He will provide the new car or whatever when we need it.

I think many of us are just like the goats looking at the greener grass in someone else's yard and straining to get it. The odd thing is someone is probably sitting in their house looking at you and wishing they had your things. What we all need to do is to appreciate the good things we have and stop worrying about the things we don't have.

The Lost Cat

My neighbor's cat got out of the house Friday evening. This cat, named "Gabby" for his constant "talking", is not used to being outside. In fact, the only other time he got out he was lost for more than a day. A number of neighbors pitched in on Friday night trying to help find the cat. The last time I saw him, he was running across the street into a large field.

Everybody gave up Friday evening assuming that he would come home when he got hungry or when it got dark. That particular Friday night we had a great deal of rain. I called my neighbor on Saturday morning expecting some good news, but I was disappointed. I got dressed and decided to venture out into the briar field where I last saw Gabby. I spent several hours walking in and around the field, calling and hoping I would find the cat.

My searches on Saturday morning, afternoon and evening all proved to be fruitless. Sunday morning I drove around the community, still searching for Gabby. I thought I spotted him, but he ran before I could get close enough to tell. All the time I was looking I was praying for the silly, yet precious cat. Gabby is particularly special to my wife and me because we nursed him to health after he was found injured as a kitten.

Sunday morning at church I found myself praying for the cat. I was having a difficult time concentrating on the message being delivered because I was thinking so much about Gabby. One of the things the speaker was encouraging us to do was seek the Lord and press into Him. I agreed with the speaker and immediately prayed again for Gabby. Then I felt the Lord ask me in my spirit if I was seeking him and his presence as much as I was seeking this little cat.

That was a tough question, but the honest truth was "No." Don't misunderstand me, I have been praying and reading the word regularly. The truth is, I have not sought His presence recently as I have challenged each of you to do. You see, it is easy to talk and write about such things but it is difficult to get the flesh to follow through.

It is rewarding to seek the Lord, because he will usually let you find him. However, once you find him he will change you, and that's the part that we all hate. Nobody likes change. Nobody likes to think that they need to change but the truth is, following Christ demands constant change. When the Spirit of the Lord fills your life and you give him control, there will be change.

While we are all afraid of change, I want to remind you how good it is when God is in control of it. When we make His changes things are always better. You see, God knows what he is doing. He is getting all the bad things out of our lives. As I heard it in a song, "He's changing me from my earthly things to the heavenly." So you see the changes are for the good, we just have to let God do them.

I learned one other thing about the Lord through this search for the cat. I learned that hope plays an important part of faith. While I have faith that we will find Gabby I have to keep hope alive or my faith may be defeated. What is hope? It is a cherished desire that what you expect will be fulfilled. Hope is also a trust. Who do we as Christians have our hope in? Our hope is in Jesus; we must trust the Lord. .

Paul writes in I Corinthians 13:13, "And now these three remain: faith, hope and love. But the greatest of these is love." We must believe God, trust him with our lives even if it does mean change and love him whole-heartedly.

Press into him whole-heartedly. God desires that we seek his face diligently like I sought the neighbor's cat. God wants fellowship with us, his sons and daughters, because we are precious to Him. Let me encourage you to seek the Lord with an unwavering faith in Him. Trust Him completely because He is the source of all hope. Fill your hearts to overflowing with His unconditional love. Then, share that love with others.

This is a drawing of Gabby, done by Bridgett McBride.

Faith to Believe

If you have the faith as small as a mustard see,
you can say to this mountain,
'move from here to there' and it will move.
Nothing will be impossible for you!
Matthew 17:20

Two weeks ago I wrote about my neighbor's lost cat. The cat wondered away on a Friday evening. Many neighbors worked hard to try to find the cat. For over two weeks we had very little luck. There were occasional sightings to encourage our faith. Finally, this past Monday a neighbor spotted Gabby and was about to catch him. He had lost a bit of weight and he smelled pretty bad, but other than that he appeared to be fine. Thank the Lord!

Anyone who has a pet will understand the joy that was felt by everyone once we had found Gabby. After all this cold weather we had begun to lose faith that we would find him alive. Even with our weak faith we continued to pray for Gabby. Now that he is home safe and sound we have been rejoicing.

This has reminded me of the story of the lost sheep. You know the story. The shepherd is watching his sheep and then he notices that one sheep is missing. He gets up and leaves the ninety-nine others and goes off to search for the one lost sheep. It says he will rejoice more over the one lost sheep that he finds more than over the ninety-nine that stayed together.

It always puzzled me why he would leave the ninety-nine alone to go searching for the one lost sheep. I always thought that he should stay and protect the ones that stayed together and the heck with the lost one. The shepherd illustrates the heart of God toward us by leaving the group to go in search of the one lost sheep. We were lost before Jesus came searching for us. Thank the Lord he did not give up on us before he found us.

I have also come to understand the heart of Jesus in the search for the lost sheep. I prayed hard for this little cat while he was missing. I think I prayed every day and on many days I was praying several times a day. The scriptures say that Jesus is interceding to the Father on our behalf. I think he is also interceding on behalf of the lost.

My neighbor's cat had been spotted several times by different people but he was not allowing himself to be caught. Jesus searches for his children, hoping that they will allow themselves to be found. They make occasional appearances in church, or talk briefly with his children, but right when He is about to catch them they run away. I do not understand why people run away from God. I guess they are frightened just like the cat. They do not understand that God wants to take care of them. He will give them a better life. God wants to be their friend. He wants to be our friend.

Jesus tells the parable of the lost sheep right after he has rebuked the disciples for not allowing the children to come to him. He taught his disciples not to look down on children because their angels always see the face of the Father. It is comforting to know that God has assigned angels to watch over us. It is amazing to know that God sees these angels face to face all the time.

God's angels are keeping watch over us. Even while we were lost God had angels assigned to us to watch over us. God wants to reveal himself to everyone, but there are many who run away from God just like the cat ran away from its owner. God does not force Himself on anyone, He waits to be invited in to their lives.

I encourage you to open your heart to God. He yearns to spend time with each one of his children. We are all precious in God's sight. To those who are close, stay that way as you walk with the Lord through life. To those who have wandered away, come on home because God wants to be your shepherd.

Good-bye Old Friend

I know I have written much about animals lately. Today, I feel the need to write a tribute to a very special pet that is no longer with us. My mother's dog, Kringle, is now running and playing in that huge back yard in the sky. If you'll permit, I would like to share his story.

My parents separated just over 11 years ago in early November. For Christmas my mother decided to get my little sister, who was still at home, a puppy. My mother felt it would be a comfort to my little sister during that difficult time in her life. Our neighbors at the time had a Maltese puppy. This type of dog is normally small, from two to seven pounds. The puppy my mother chose was the runt of a litter of purebred parents.

The puppy arrived on Christmas morning. My sister names him Sir Kris Kringle. My mother believes God sent Kringle on a major assignment. His orders were to love the Creamer family unconditionally. Mom thinks that because he had such a big job, God made Kringle bigger than normal. In time, this runt grew to a whopping eleven pounds.

I believe that God does use animals in people's lives. There are scriptural examples to support my theory. Think about Balaam the prophet who was protected from the angel by his donkey. Then the donkey spoke to Balaam. Remember when Daniel was thrown in the lions' den? The next day the king couldn't wait to see if the Lord had spared Daniel. The king was glad when he saw his friend. Then the king ordered the men who set Daniel up to be thrown into the lions' den. These men were killed by the lions before they even hit the floor of the den.

Today animals are being used to help mentally ill patients, hardened criminals, and the elderly. I wonder if animals might be angels in disguise. Animals have a way of showing unconditional love. I think many of us could learn some lessons from animals. I have to yell at our cats occasionally because they are doing something they shouldn't. Then after a while they come around purring and wanting to be petted, showing their love.

I can imagine the conversation that might have taken place

between the angel of the Lord and Kringle when God was going to give him his assignment. "Are you willing to go to the Creamer household? It's a big job."

"I'm the smallest dog in the litter. Maybe God needs a bigger dog to get the job done. I would sure hate to fail the Lord." Kringle answered.

"The Lord will equip you to do the things he is calling you to do. Your part is accepting his love and calling then walking in obedience," the angel replies. Taking a deep breath, Kringle weighed the options in his mind, he considered the challenge, and then he took the assignment.

I think the call of God occurs in a similar way in our lives. Most of us don't get lucky enough to have angels calling us. However, God does have a purpose for each one of us. When we find out what it is we may feel frightened of unable to fulfill it, but that is normal. The Lord calls us to do things that will cause us to be dependent on him. That way when we accomplish it there will be no room for pride.

God's call for us is to walk by faith. We walk by faith when we accept God's love and allow it to work through us. God will enable, he will work through us. We have to offer our skills, abilities, and our lives to him so he can work out his purposes in us and through us. An obedient man or woman who allows God's love to flow through him or her will accomplish much for the kingdom of God.

As for Kringle, he fulfilled God's purposes for his life. He loved the Creamer family during a time when love seemed to be on vacation. I know I will miss my little pal when I go home to see my mother. But I know when I go home to see my Father in Heaven he will be there. Good-bye Kringle my dear friend, I will miss you.

This is a drawing of Sir Kris Kringle done by Bridgett McBride.

Persistent as a Bird

I have noticed lots of little birds around North Stanly since I started teaching there. This past fall there was a big effort to clean all the bird nests from the outside bells and to get them working. Once the bells were cleaned out they built wire cages around them to keep the birds from making nests again. It seemed they had been successful.

The other day I was walking around campus and heard that wonderful sound of baby birds begging for food. Those babies were peeping away like crazy. Since I could hear their cries so clearly I wanted to see the nest. Guess where I found it? Yes, it was in one of the bells. This little mother bird had managed to squeeze herself past the wire mesh to get that old nesting spot back. I stood and watched laughing in amazement.

That little bird had to be persistent to get that spot back again. That got me to thinking about several other birds that have shown the same quality. There is a mother robin who has a nest at the front door to the *Stanly News & Press*. She doesn't like you to stop and stare. I have a mother starling who built her nest in my shed last year. It was in the rafters and she stayed out of my way so I left her alone. Little did I know, I was starting a tradition; she is back again this year.

My mother-in-law has a robin that has tried for several years to have a nest on her front porch light. The bird starts to build and my mother-in-law pushes the beginning parts of the nest off. So the mother robin persistently tries to start again, but my mother-in-law pushes it off again. The two came to a truce last year when the bird made her nest over the garage door light. I asked my mother-in-law the other day if her robin was back this year. She said "Yes, but at the wrong light again." Persistence!

If only we as Christians had that kind of persistence. We commit our lives to Christ and we feel his call on us to serve him. We anxiously run after him as a young lover chases his love. Then it happens, we meet resistance. We know the Lord is calling us to do something, but it just doesn't seem to be working out. That's when we need persistence.

Persistence is that quality that causes faith to rise up within us. Doubts and fears may try to stop us but we press on. Failures may line the road making us feel unworthy of the call in our lives. God knows that we will fail along the way. When Jesus bought us on the cross 2000 years ago, He bought us failures and all. It is God's heart that we persistently push pass the failure to answer our call in life. Sometimes the way seems unclear, almost impossible, but we must press on.

In Luke 18:1-8, Jesus spoke of persistence in the parable about a widow. The widow went to the judge asking for justice. She was denied. She persisted and continued to ask even when she was turned down. Finally, the judge decided to give her justice. Jesus encourages us to be like the widow in our prayers. We should pray persistently.

This should teach us something important about the Lord. I believe God has a plan about how certain events are going to take place; predestination, if you will. But I also believe that as children of God we can influence God's heart. How? Through intercessory prayer. God may have decided that something is going to occur in a particular way. I sincerely believe that if we are persistent in our prayers God may be moved to change his mind. Remember, God, like any good father, wants to give his children good things. Also, keep in mind that we must not pray selfishly.

In Paul's first letter to Timothy he challenged, "Fight the good fight of the faith. Take hold of the eternal life to which you were called..." Living our life on earth will be a fight sometimes. God is looking for his children to be persistent. So like the birds, go out there and fight persistently. You'll win!

Bird Hunt

I have a bird's nest in my shed. They found a way in through the end and they seem to be happy. I don't mind them being there because it is fun to watch and listen to them. My only problem with them is that the parents use the inside as a practice flying zone and you can only imagine what they do in there.

Well, yesterday morning I was heading out to do some errands. I needed to go to the shed for something before I left. When I opened the door four baby birds scrambled out of my way. They were all squawking and running around. It was obvious that they had not learned to fly yet. All I could think was, "What are they going to do?" I decided that I had to intervene.

I got my gardening gloves and I cleared the way to get my ladder next to where the nest sits. Then I began the process of chasing the birds. They really squawked when I started to chase them. I could just imagine the mother returning to all the screaming birds and starting to attack me. I think you get the picture; it was a circus.

I got three of the baby birds into the nest. One of them had been seriously injured in the fall and I later discovered that he didn't make it. The other two seemed content to be home, although they continued to squawk. I thought, "Alright, just this one last bird and I'll be done". The last one seemed to have caught himself in a corner and I thought he would be an easy catch.

The last bird was the largest and healthiest of the four. He wasn't an easy catch because he fought me harder than the others. But being bigger and more persistent, I won. I stepped up the ladder and placed him gingerly back in to the nest. I guess I should clarify that there are two entrances to this nest. One is from the outside, the other, from inside my shed. The nest sits in the overhang from the roof up in the rafters. I never got around to sealing up the shed so they come in the ends. If I leave the main door open they will fly in and out of it too. I was using the inside entrance to place them back in the nest.

When I let this last bird go he immediately ran out the other hole. So I ran to the outside, and there he was, running around on the ground. I looked up at the main hole and here was the weak bird about to fall out, too. Plop, he landed on the ground. I ran inside the shed and retrieved the ladder. I got the bird that looked weak and put him back in the nest first. Then I started after the strong bird, who took one look at me and made a beeline right under the shed.

This began another round of trying to get him out. I had to get a flashlight and a big stick. Before I could begin trying to get him out, I had to trim the weeds from around the building. It needed it, anyway. I looked and looked and I couldn't see the bird under there. I decided I needed a break and I sat down on the porch with a cool drink.

As I sat there on the porch it dawned on me to pray for the little bird. I prayed several prayers while trying to catch the little birds; "Oh God, PLEASE don't let that mother come back now and start pecking me on the head!" "Please let me catch these birds so I can get out of here." Those were offered in haste, and I thought that now that I was calmer maybe I should offer a calmer prayer. I prayed, "Father please help me find that little bird". Instantly I felt as though the Lord said, "OK."

With faith rekindled I struck out to find this little bird. I started in the garden thinking maybe he ran there when I wasn't paying attention. No luck. I looked under the shed again from every angle, still no luck. Finally, I rolled over and looked up at the sky. "God," I said, "you told me to go look and that I would find this little bird. I felt it in my spirit. Now where do I look?" I know I was complaining, but I wasn't mad at God. I just wanted to help the little bird.

I felt a nudge in the spirit. "Look again." So I rolled over and looked again. "I don't see anything." I said out loud, as if God was standing right there. "Are you sure?" I could almost imagine him saying. "Yeah. You want me to look for your…" "Wait! I think I see a little head bobbing!" I got the flashlight and looked closer. Yep, there he was, sitting in a little shallow spot. "Alright, God!"

I got my stick and got ready to nudge him. Just before I did I thought another little prayer might give me success. "Please help me get him out safely." Then I started with my stick ever so gently. As I got close the bird ran…in the opposite direction. "Come back here you crazy little bird. Can't you see I'm trying to help you?" After several more failed attempts I gave up.

I sat down on the porch and tried to sort through things for an answer. As I sat quietly, I felt the Lord beginning to teach me some valuable lessons through this experience. Each bird seem to symbolize the lost and their response to the gospel. Remember that we as the church have something that will help the lost. We also have the responsibility to share it with them, BUT... we are not responsible for their response to the gospel.

The little bird that was weak and hurt from the fall represents those who will never respond to the gospel. They have been wounded by the world and will never look to the Heavenly Father. Even though I believe every person is reachable with the gospel of hope, many will never respond because of deep-seated pain and rejection. This is a sad reality because if they only knew how much God loved them and how badly he wanted to heal them, they might respond.

The two birds that stayed put in the nest are those that receive the gospel of hope. They stay in the church where they will get fed and one day they will strike out on their own, when the time is right. They will grow up into adults and be able to reproduce, meaning they will be able to attract new converts and disciple them into Christians.

Now the little bird that was stronger and hid under the shed, he's harder to place. I think he closely resembles our young adults. He's strong because he has stayed in the church and eaten plenty of good food. He is almost ready to fly, but not quite. The desire to be independent is strong but he is not ready yet. When adults come up alongside to help them, they resist. They think they know all the answers. What they do not realize is that Satan, like the neighborhood cat, is looking for lunch.

I think we also have to realize that sometimes they do not want any help. We can't force anyone to accept help if they do not want it. Teenagers and adults are more alike in this matter. Someone has to decide they want help before help will be effective. It's like in Alcoholics Anonymous; you have to admit you are an alcoholic before you can change.

What is the solution? How do we help? All I think adults can do for our youth and young adults when they seem anxious to fly, is to stand ready to help. We need to pray for their personal safety and that God will complete the good work he began in their lives. We also have to remember that if we train a child in the way he should go, when he is old he will not depart from it. That does not say that he won't depart from it in his young adult life. That is why adults need to pray for the youth and young adults.

I decided to leave my little bird alone for a while. He would come out when he was hungry. So last evening I walked out to the shed and there was the bird. I tried once again to catch him. A neighbor came to help corner this little sucker. He moved fast and he seemed strong. Well, I finally caught the little guy and got him back up to his nest. I told him to stay calm that he was home and I gently laid him in the nest. My neighbor was on the outside and I was climbing down from the ladder and I heard him say, "Oh, there's your little bird again. He's out here on the ground."

"Oh, no!" I thought.

"Oops, there he goes under your shed."

And that is exactly where I left that little stinker. I did see him this morning. He was under the hole to the nest wailing away for mamma. Many people treat the church the same way this bird is treating his nest. They want the food and comfort the nest provides but they do not want to live within its limits. So they leave the nest and wander around wailing for help and direction in life.

Our response to this type of person must be to help. They may act like my little bird did and run away from us. We still need to keep reaching out with the gospel of love to the wandering few who do not have a home. Some day if the enemy doesn't eat them they will learn to fly and will come to realize their need for the Lord and will return.

There is a somewhat funny ending to my story about the bird. I was sitting on the porch about lunch time the same day that I saw him calling from under the shed. He was calling out clear as a bell still. Then I looked up and on top of my shed were about ten to fifteen adult birds. They were all talking up a storm to each other. I watched as one by one the birds would walk down the roof of the shed and look over at the baby bird on the ground. They would look at him from several angles and then walk up the roof talking up a storm. Each bird did the same thing. It was like they were trying to figure out how they were going to rescue the baby.

Finally, after each bird had a look they all came together for one last conference. After the conference the birds began flying away two at a time in all different directions. They all flew away until there was only two left and they stayed up there together for quite a while. I never have figured out what went on, but it sure was comical to watch.

I only saw the baby bird once more after that. I never figured out if he learned to fly or became someone's lunch. I hope he learned to fly.

If you are needing a touch from God don't run from Him, run to Him. I promise He will accept you with open arms and He will hide you under his protective wings. God loves you.

Flying High

**but those who hope in the Lord
will renew their strength,
They will soar on wings like eagles;
they will run and not grow weary,
they will walk and not faint.**
Isaiah 40:31

I know I have told you about the starlings that have nested in my shed. Well, the question comes to mind; how do they learn to fly? For that matter, how does any bird learn to fly? I know that the mother starling gives her babies flight training in my shed. It must scare the ---- out of the birds to learn to fly. The evidence of that is all over the floor of my shed!

I have recently learned how a mother eagle teacher her babies to fly. The mother will push the baby off the nest and then dive under the baby, catching it on her back. Then the mother proceeds to climb high into the sky. The baby bird sits on the mother's back while she climbs higher and higher. When the mother is about a mile or more above the ground she flips over and drops the baby in the air.

The baby, who has never flown before, begins dropping like a rock. The wind rushes through the baby's wings as it is squalling for its mother. Then an amazing thing begins to happen. The baby tries to pull its wings in close to its body but the wind from the downward tumble keeps pulling them away. The baby begins to flap feverishly, usually not too much avail.

The mother, in the meantime, circles around her falling baby. She is careful to protect it from other predator birds as the baby makes the free fall to the ground. The mother keeps that watchful eye on her baby. Then, just in the nick of time, the mother swoops in and catches her baby on her back. Then the mother once again begins to climb higher and higher to repeat the process.

In this way the baby learns to flap its wings and before too many days it learns to fly. The basic need to survive teaches the baby bird how to fly. That's the first of many things that must be learned, because flying is only a basic skill. There is still the need to hone the skills and to learn evasive maneuvers, diving and hunting techniques. But if the mother is unwilling to put the baby through these life-threatening situations the baby will not learn to fly or survive on its own.

I believe many parents fail to give their children these kinds of experiences. When parents see their children going through something tough they run to their defense wanting to protect them from the hurt. What the parent needs to do is just love the child and be there for them.

I imagine that it is difficult for the mother eagle to hear her child's plaintiff cries for help and not respond. The mother knows that these difficult lessons will cause her baby to grow up strong. I can also imagine the baby popping Mom in the head when it gets picked up near the ground. It probably says all kinds of terrible things in bird language too.

"Hey Mom, what did you do that for?" he pops her in the head for emphasis. "Are you trying to kill me or something? If you are mad at me, just tell me. Hey, if it's that fish thing, Brian did that. Hey Mom, this sure is a beautiful world from way up here." He continues while Mom circles around, getting higher and higher. "I love getting a ride on your shoulders, Mom. I'm sorry for all that stuff I said before, but you sure scared me dropping me like that. Wow, it looks like you could see forever from way up herrrrrreeee! MMMMMMoooooooommmmmmmm …. hhhhhheeeeellllppppppp!" Away the baby bird goes falling downward again. Yet the mother knows what it has to do and is determined to do it.

The lessons of life can be difficult to learn. Our response as adults can be to shield our children (or in my case, my students) from learning the lessons, or let them learn the lessons the hard way. Couldn't the mother bird just tell her children how to fly and save them the trouble of falling from such a great height? No. The only way to learn is to fall through the sky. Necessity can teach us some things really fast.

If you feel you are going through some tough lessons in life remember the Lord is with you. He, like the mother bird, is circling around you protecting you from predators and allowing you to learn the lesson. When you feel yourself falling, turn to the Lord and see if you can learn what to do so you will be able to learn the lesson faster. First, you have to stretch out your wings and learn to flap. Soon, if you keep trying, you will be able to fly. Good luck, Ace.

The angel of the Lord encamps around
those who fear him,
and he delivers them.
Psalm 34:7

Work

Do not work for food that spoils, but for food that endures to
eternal life, which the Son of Man will give you.
John 6:27

Work

*Whatever you do, work at it with all your heart,
as working for the Lord, not for men, since you know
you will receive an inheritance from the Lord as a reward.*
Colossians 3:23 & 24

Work

*And God blessed the seventh day and made it holy, because on it
he rested from all the work of creating that he had done.*
Genesis 2: 3
If God rested on the seventh day, shouldn't we?

School Prayer

I can remember high school graduation almost as if it was yesterday. I graduated in a very large auditorium in the middle of a class of about six hundred. North Stanley High school's total enrollment is only about six hundred. I can clearly remember how nervous I was hoping that stupid hat would stay on my head. As they called out my name, I remember my little sister yelling out, "Alright Doug!!" It was a little embarrassing, but the love she expressed was much appreciated and well received.

There are two other major things that I remember about the graduation ceremony itself. One, Chuck Robb, who was a candidate for the Governor of Virginia, was the commencement speaker. (I graduated from Kempsville High School in Virginia Beach, Virginia.) Ironically, four years later, when I graduated from James Madison University, Governor Robb was the commencement speaker again. The second thing I remember about graduating, and the most important, was my pastor gave both the opening and closing word of prayer.

I had no idea when I arrived at graduation that he was going to be there. I can remember how excited I got when they introduced him. I nearly leapt out of my chair, and I told those around me that he was my pastor. They were not impressed and probably did not care. But I was so proud that he had been selected to pray for us. I believe God's presence filled the place as he led us in prayer. It was very special walking up to the platform to receive my diploma because the first person I saw was my pastor. He smiled and nodded at me as they called out my name. He exuded a sense of pride as I walked up to receive my diploma.

The memory of my pastor leading us in prayer fills me with joy. I am also glad we invited God there through a word of prayer. At the same time there is a pain of sorrow that touches my heart, too. Why you may ask? Because our Supreme Court, in all its wisdom, has passed a new law that restricts prayer from graduation and other ceremonies. That means the students will not be able to have the special kind of memory or feelings that prayer provides at such times.

There is only one loop hole, a mere thread of hope that will allow prayer to continue to be a part of school functions. It will take young people with backbone and courage to bring prayer back. The new law allows for student led prayer. If students initiate the prayer, then it will be legal. Well young people, it will take courage, leadership and guts, but I am convinced you can do it.

It is a shame that we adults have allowed out country to wonder so far from the Lord. With this law, we have almost kicked God completely out of the public schools. What we really need now is for people who do believe in the power of prayer to pray for our schools. God help us and God help the young people who will have to stand up for prayer if it is to happen. There are two small seeds of hope in this situation. The first is that God can do exceedingly abundantly beyond all that we ask or think. The second is a very simple passage of scripture that comes to mind and builds hope within my spirit in this particular situation. The scripture is,

"… and a little child shall lead them."

The prayer of a righteous man (or woman)
is powerful and effective.
James 5:16

Graduation Prayer 1994

On Friday we send a new group of teenagers out into the world. It's graduation time. Those seniors are biting at the bit and we teachers are ready for them to go. No offense intended, but I think we are all tired and ready to see the end of the school year.

I have attended every graduation since I began teaching almost nine years ago. Each graduation is special and unique. The graduation of the class of 1994 will be no different. I am sure the civic center will be packed to watch this momentous event. My only concern about this graduation is that one invitation has not and will not be sent.

Once again this program has been nicely laid out. There are guest speakers, awards, scholarships and of course the diplomas. There is one thing missing, an invitation to God to come and bless the proceedings. There will be no prayers on the program. Prayer has been legislated out of the proceedings. Imagine that, in a nation where freedom of speech is protected, we can't say a simple prayer to invite God to graduation. At a very important time in the lives of our youth, God is left outside.

Why can't a minister come and offer a word of prayer like one did when I graduated? The disturbing answer to this question is simple, because someone objected to it and called a law suit. Isn't it amazing that in a democratic society we no longer do things that the majority want? I believe that the majority of people in Stanly County would like a prayer spoken at graduation. But a small minority said they would be offended, so we will not have prayer.

I think it is important that we be sensitive to those whose faith is different from ours. If they would prefer that we said, "May God bless these proceedings." and keep the name of Jesus out, that would be alright. Do you see that is not a compromise, but rather it is being sensitive to those with different beliefs? Jesus would always be sensitive to others because the lost won't be won through disrespect.

Last year I was proud of the seniors from North Stanly for standing up together and saying the Lord's Prayer. Though some did it just to be disrespectful to authority, I believe many did it because they felt prayer was an important part of graduation and they wanted to express their faith. In any case it shows a desire on the part of our youth to seek the Lord, and I believe God will honor that.

The tough question I have asked myself is what would I pray if given the chance. I believe my prayer would go something like:

Dear Heavenly Father, I thank you for bringing these young adults to this place in their lives. I thank you for keeping them safe and for helping them to accomplish the things necessary for graduation. I thank you for the trials they have endured and the lessons they have learned. Father, I thank you for each one and the part they play in making the whole of the Class of 1994.

Father, as they are about to embark on life's journey, I pray that You would grant them spiritual guidance. Grant them strength to climb the mountains. Give them endurance to walk through the valleys. Lead them down the roads that You have designed for them. Teach them to hold onto hope in the low times so their faith will endure. Help them to resist the temptation that the easy road offers.

Father, help them to keep their eyes on You. Cause them to lay up treasure in heaven, for that is the true and lasting reward. Help them to serve others because in serving others true leaders are born. Give them conviction to live by their word. Give them the courage to chase their dreams and to pursue excellence. Help them to accomplish Your purposes in the earth for there is no greater call in life.

Father, as they strike out to seek their fame and fortune, help them to find their faith, hope and love. I pray that their future would be placed in Your mighty hands. Amen.

Persecution is a Good Thing

All authority in heaven and on earth has been given to me. Therefore go and make disciples of all the nations, baptizing them in the name of the Father and of the Son and of the Holy Spirit, and teaching them to obey everything I have commanded you. And surely I will be with you always, to the very end of the age.
Matthew 28:18-20

You know young people can really surprise you sometimes. Adults can occasionally speak harshly of the younger generation, but I saw something that would have made them proud. I went to our high school graduation. I found people there who acted like fools, however, I did see something there that warmed my spirit and it made me proud of our youth.

What was it that got my attention at graduation? It was three speeches given by three graduating seniors. The Senior Class President led the group by inviting the Lord's presence to the ceremony. If you will recall, I shared my concern last week that prayer would not be a part of graduation.

The Salutatorian and the Valedictorian both spoke openly of their personal faith in Jesus Christ. They expressed gratitude to the Lord for bringing them to this point in their lives. It takes a lot of guts to get up and express faith so boldly, in front of your peers, let alone the crowd that filled the Agri-Civic Center.

I wonder if these three individuals would have been so bold if a pastor had been there to say a prayer. I wonder if their speeches would have been different. Would they have been willing to take such a stand if circumstances had been different? Is this an example of persecution?

Persecution according to my Webster means to suffer because of your belief or religion. Is the government harassing Christians by passing a law that does not allow prayer at graduation? I believe that it is. I believe that this is a type of persecution. I also believe that the persecution of these students has caused them to become more out spoken about their beliefs. Is it possible that something that seems bad on the surface does some good?

I have noticed more students wearing Christian T-shirts to school. The students are willing to take a public stand for their faith, which I believe will cause them to be stronger. So the result of the persecution is stronger and less inhibited Christians who are unashamed of the gospel. That sounds great to me.

We have all heard the Great Commission read to us in church. How many of us actively go about fulfilling it? Do we take a stand in our place of work? I don't mean a rash disrespectful stand that runs people away. I'm talking about the kind of firm stance that lets others know you are a Christian. Do you ever tell others you are praying for them and concerned about them? Do you stand up for what is right and live ethically? Are you an example of the mercy and love of God? That's taking the Great Commission to work.

What about in your neighborhood? Are you a servant to those who live around you? Do you share with them the love of God? If Jesus is truly the most important person in your life, don't you think you should talk to others about him? Do you remember what Jesus said would happen if we did not confess his name to those around us? He said that he would not confess us before the Father. I think that means he wants us to witness to our neighbors and those at work.

What if we don't? I think God will bring some kind of persecution our way to cause us to come out of our shell. Why do I believe that? When Jesus gave the Great Commission he said to GO! What did the disciples do? They stayed until ... they were persecuted. Then they went out from Jerusalem in all directions sharing the gospel as they went.

So I guess that means we have a choice. We can start sharing the gospel where God has us, or we can wait until God sends some persecution. I don't know how you feel about persecution, but I prefer to share without it; thank-you very much.

I am proud of the seniors who met the persecution straight on and stood up for their faith. Their reward shall be great in heaven. Let's hope we can follow in their footsteps.

In fact, when we were with you,
we kept telling you we would be persecuted.
And it turned out that way as you well know.
I Thessalonians 3:4

In fact, everyone who wants to live a godly
life in Christ Jesus will be persecuted.
2 Timothy 3:12

Memory

**Do not let this Book of the Law depart from
your mouth; meditate on it day and night,
so that you will be careful to do everything
written in it. Then you will be
prosperous and successful.**
Joshua 1:8

I am going to be doing one of my favorite things in this week,
act. The faculty at North Stanly in conjunction with the drama
department are putting on a play. It is fun to put on a play, but it is
a good bit of work too. This will be my fourth faculty play. I
always seem to get good roles that are enjoyable. I have played a
hotel desk clerk, a mild mannered superman type, a bumbling
Sherlock Holmes, and, this year, I will be Dracula.

Part of the reason I enjoy acting so much is that it is an
opportunity to have fun with the faculty members. We always pick
a comedy and add more funny lines to it. The biggest part of
preparing for a play is memorizing all the lines. Last year's play
required the most memorization that I had ever attempted. And
yes, I did mess up some of my lines! This year we are doing a
shorter play with fewer lines, which is a good thing for me with my
busy schedule.

All the memorization has caused me to reflect on the lack of
work I have put into memorizing God's word. I once complained to
a friend that I could not memorize anything, especially God's
word. The stark reality is, if I can remember my lines for the play
in front of all those people, then I ought to be able to memorize
God's word. I think God has been gently reminding me that I need
to work on this part of my life.

The question that surfaces in my mind is why would God want
me to memorize his word? The reason is not so I can just repeat it.
We need to keep in mind that the devil himself knows and can
quote the scriptures. Remember he quoted scripture to Jesus when
he was tempting him. The purpose is not and cannot be for mere

repetition.

There are two purposes for scripture memory. One is to help us stand up against temptation. Remember how Jesus resisted temptation, he quoted God's word to the devil. We need to put this into practice so we can stand the testing of our faith and temptation.

The second purpose for scripture memory is meditation. Now I know this word can open the proverbial "can of worms." I must clarify myself and say that I am not speaking of eastern mysticism or transcendental meditation. It is my personal opinion that these are not of the Lord. What I am speaking about is a deliberate reflection upon, focused thoughts about, or the pondering of spiritual truths.

You know how you read a particular passage of scripture several times and nothing seems to stand out. Then one time you read the same passage and something grabs your attention; it speaks to you. If this comes from a few moments of contemplation on God's word than that is a meditation. We should memorize God's word so that we can think about it and allow it to speak to us.

God, through the Holy Spirit, will bring back to our memory passages of scripture to help us in difficult times or situations. He desires to help us understand ourselves, the place we are in life, and the destination we are pursuing. God also desires to reveal Himself and to help us understand His ways.

Psalm 119 is the longest Psalm in the Bible, and it is full of reasons why we should meditate on and memorize God's word. For example, it makes us wiser than our enemies, gives us understanding, and keeps us from the devil's traps. It is filled with good promises; it's encouraging; it's also convicting, and it is a light unto our paths. I encourage you to dig into God's word. It's a source of life, and it will help you to stand in the day in which we live.

Here Comes the Judge

I am once again acting in the faculty & student play at North Stanly. By the time you read this we will have done our final performance. The setting for the play is a courtroom. I am a wacky judge who shoots off a bunch of one liners (if I can remember my lines). The cast is full of wonderful characters that provide one laugh right after another.

One of the students in the play, who is also a reader, asked what type of column was going to come out of the play. I had not thought about the prospect until she asked me about it. I wasn't sure you could get anything special out of this comical and wacky play.

The judge does have several straight lines that make up the moral of the play. The judge tells one plaintiff that true crimes are committed in the heart. Jesus certainly agreed with that idea. Sin begins in the mind and the heart. Jesus said that it was what came out of a man or woman's heart that makes them unclean. They include such things as greed, lust, idolatry, hate and gossip.

The judge also says that thinking that you are better than somebody else is a real crime. Jesus believed this and showed us by example that he meant it. He was found with the well to do and with the outcasts of society. When the woman cried at Jesus's feet, He was sitting in a Pharisee's house. It was probably one of the nicest homes in the city. Yet in that place he reached out to the prostitute whose heart was repentant. He wasn't afraid of what others might think if he reached out to help this poor woman. He isn't or wasn't concerned with image or status.

In this one example, Jesus shows us he is willing to reach out to anyone no matter who they might be. He identifies with people from all walks of life. If you are rich, he will be rich to reach you. If you are poor and outcast, He will be likewise to reach you. Jesus desires to show his love and compassion to everyone.

There is one other thing that struck me about the play that I think is worth thinking about. One day we will all stand before the judge to be judged for the way we live our lives. I can say that I am glad that Jesus will not be like the judge that I play in this production. I don't think the judgement will be a pleasant time because everything we do will be reviewed. I am glad that Jesus will be a merciful judge, if I repent for my sins.

When the judgement does come I know that Satan the accuser will be there proclaiming all the reasons I do not deserve eternal life. The truth is he will be right. I do not deserve eternal life in heaven. Thank God that I have a Savior who can deliver me from such an accuser.

I guess if Satan is the prosecutor than Jesus would be compared to the public defender. After Stan comes up with all the reasons I do not deserve to go to heaven, Jesus will stand up and make my defense. Jesus will say to the Judge, his Father, (I love it! Do you think that Jesus will have any pull with the judge who happens to be his Father?) Anyway he will say, "This one is mine. I bought him with my blood on the cross. All his sins are forgiven." The Father will answer, "The accused will stand." Then He will look straight into your eyes and say, "Well done good and faithful servant. Enter heaven."

Imagine hearing those precious words, particularly when you imagine you don't deserve them. There is nothing any of us can do to earn heaven. It is the free gift of God. We only have to reach out and receive it while there is still time.

I know when I stand before the judge I will be glad to know that Jesus is in my corner. I encourage you to be sure he is in your corner. I also challenge you to be a willing servant who will share that gift with those around you. We live in a needy world, a world full of people who need THE public defender standing beside them in the Day of Judgement.

The Fair Judgement

**They will also answer, (That's not fair!!) "Lord,
when did we see you hungry or thirsty or a stranger
or needing clothes or sick or in prison, and did not help you?"
He will reply, "I tell you the truth,
whatever you did not do for one of the least of these,
you did not do for me."**
Matthew 25:44 & 45

Every classroom teacher who reads this will identify with the following statement. "That was not fair." Don't tell my principal, but the truth is I have heard it myself. We don't want to be unfair; it just seems that way to the students. But I guarantee you the students let me know right away when they think I have been unfair.

What's my response to them? First, I try to listen to their complaint. If their complaint is not valid they will hear, "That's too bad, I'm the teacher." There has to be rules and limits and I, as a teacher, have to enforce them. I learned that from my parents. If I complained that life was not fair, my mother would respond, "This is my house, and it doesn't have to be fair." or "This is my house, and you'll do as I tell you." I remember thinking that it really didn't seem fair.

The question of fairness has run through my mind all week. It all started when one of the kids in children's church told me that, "God's not fair. He's just." He is a God of justice, not necessarily fairness. My initial reaction was to correct the child. However, I decided to stay quiet and meditate on it before I corrected her. The truth is a week later and I think she is right and I am wrong.

One thing I considered was eternal life. If God was fair and gave us what we deserved, we would all have a "HOT" future, eternally speaking. I am hoping that God will be just with me. Through His justice and mercy done on the cross, he will allow us to enter heaven.

Jesus illustrated this justice through the parable of the sheep and the goats. Jesus said that at the last judgement he would divide the people into two groups. To the group on his left, he will tell them to depart from his presence forever. This group will ask why they are being sent away. The answer will be that they did not look after the needs of those around them. This group will immediately respond, "That's not fair! We always looked out for the needs of those around us." His answer will be, "When you didn't do it for the least of these you didn't do it for me."

Then He will invite the group on His right hand into the kingdom. They will ask God why they deserve heaven. The Lord's answer will be, they had looked after the needs of "the least of these." They will then enter heaven even though they did not feel worthy of such a great gift.

Who are the "least of these?" They are poor widows, single mothers, children of divorced parents, the homeless in our streets. They are the orphans in places like Romania and Albania who are left to fend for themselves. They are the AIDS babies, people living in nursing homes. They are the Serbs and Africans dying of starvation. They are those who are hurting and crying out to a merciful God for help.

Will there be hope for us to be placed in the group on his right when we arrive at heaven's doors? We have one hope and his name is Jesus. Last week I wrote about the events that surrounded the capture of Jericho. There was one family that was spared when the children of Israel took Jericho. Do you remember who?

It was Rahab the prostitute and her family. Here is a woman who sold her body to men for pleasure. She was a sinner. Why would God want to spare her? God spared her because she looked out for the spies. They were the enemy to her and her city, yet she helped them. She was looking out for the "least of these".

What about Rahab's family? Imagine being her mother or father. Would you have rejected her as a person when she came and invited you to her home? Would you have accepted her invitation? Would you be able to forgive her for what she has done with her body? In order for her family to be in her house when Israel attacked Jericho they had to love and forgive her. Do you think Rahab's life was different after this experience? I bet it was. Why? Simple, because she experienced love and mercy.

God wants us to be merciful, giving, forgiving and loving to those around us. In that way we might reach out to "the least of these." Then we will receive his justice and mercy for all eternity.

But you have neglected the more important matters of the law-
justice, mercy and faithfulness.
Matthew 23:23

He has shown you, O man, what is good.
And what does the Lord require of you?
To act justly and to love mercy
and to walk humbly with your God.
Micah 6:8

Blessed are the merciful,
for they will be shown mercy.
Matthew 5:7

Talents

His master replied, "Well done, good and faithful servant! You have been faithful with a few things; I will put you in charge of many things. Come and share your master's happiness!"
Matthew 25:23

On the last day of work this year I arrived just a couple minutes after eight. As I pulled into the parking lot I noticed the art teacher painting the now famous North Stanly rock. She painted a plain background the day before. After I parked my car, I looked over to see what she was doing and I noticed that she had just begun. So I headed in and started to do the things necessary to finish up my last day.

It was about an hour and a half later that an election was held in the library. Who would go to Joe's Donut Dinette and get some donuts for a workshop that was going on in the computer lab? I won. As I was pulling out of the parking lot I noticed the art teacher just about finished with the picture on the side of the rock. I know I stared in amazement for several minutes. I couldn't believe someone could paint that beautiful picture of the sun in just an hour and a half.

As I drove away, I wished I had half her skill. I can't draw worth a hill of beans. My students laugh at my attempt at stick figures. I have to admit that I was slightly jealous of her skill. As I reflected on it farther the Lord revealed to me that I was an artist. I laughed at that thought. I knew I didn't possess those skills. What the Lord revealed to me was that I may not use a canvas (or rock) and paint brushes, but I use blank pieces of paper and words.

I know some people really get stressed out when asked to write something, normally I don't. I don't like formal things, but anything that allows for some creativity is great. Creating pictures with words is my artwork. I am an artist.

I believe that God gives talents and skills to his people to use for his kingdom. I know for some it may be stretching it, but I believe the parable of the talents is related. If you'll remember the parable of the talents is when the master gives three servants, 1, 2, and 5 talents. Each talent is worth about a thousand dollars. He leaves the servants and later returns to settle accounts. The one with 5 gives the master 10; the one with 2 gives 4; and the one with one returns the one he received. The master was pleased with the first two because they had doubled their talents, but the last one he was really mad with because he had done nothing.

When I was younger I thought that talents were skills, not money that God had given his people. I think God gives us talents that we can use or hide. I also believe he will hold us accountable to use the skills or talents he puts in our lives. I think, like the money multiplying in the parable, the talents we possess will multiply as we use them for His Kingdom.

Allow me to take this a little farther. Let's suppose you are good at small repairs. Many local churches and members of those churches could put those skills to good use. My mother-in-law is a great cook; her church has tapped that talent very often for church socials.

Your gifts and talents may include things like cleaning, organizing, artistic skills, writing, maintenance and repair, teaching, loving and caring for others, singing and praying. Whatever your skill or talent there are ways to put them to good use within the church. Also keep in mind that these skills used to bless someone outside the church might be a real witness of God's love for them.

The bottom line: I encourage you to pray and seek the Lord asking him what talents or skills you have to offer. Then seek him about how you can use those talents and skills in a way that will bless those around you.

I Disagree With You!

I was talking with a dear friend the other day when she said, "I disagree with you." Immediately I tried to figure out what was bothering her from our conversation. Then she clarified her statement, "I don't agree with something you wrote a few weeks ago in your column." The statement was made politely and respectfully then backed with facts supporting her views.

Her point of disagreement was a springboard to a wonderful discussion on how we both viewed scripture and church life. I found the discussion exciting, interesting, challenging and eye opening. We both stated our views on various biblical issues. There was an openness and honesty there as we listened and shared our different viewpoints. It was a refreshing conversation about our faith.

Discussing religious views has always been my favorite topic of conversation. I have talked to Muslims, Jews, Mormons and Jehovah Witnesses (the Witnesses visit our neighborhood several times a year.) I find people's religious beliefs fascinating. I am interested in their belief systems and the purposes for those beliefs; the why's. When in these types of discussions with those outside my faith, I never try to force my beliefs on them. I simply share my beliefs and my personal experiences. I also carefully listen to their beliefs and experiences. I have an open, honest discussion.

I also relish the chance to discuss biblical beliefs with fellow Christians. I know and have talked with people from many different denominational backgrounds. I personally find the Catholics to be the most interesting. I must confess that I am a bit more forward when I share my beliefs with fellow Christians than those outside the faith. Being strong about my convictions makes for an interesting discussion. I think it also prepares me for those opportunities to share my faith with the lost. In both situations I am careful to listen and try to understand the other person's point of view.

I think we have lost the skill of listening. We aren't interested in another's point of view because we are preoccupied with our own. Someone else may have a different point of view about a passage of scripture that might be valid. We have to remember that God reveals himself differently to each individual that invites Him into his or her heart. Why? Simply because each of us comes to God with our own problems, hang ups, baggage, background and experiences. We are all unique and God deals with us that way.

Now be careful that you don't read into this that you should be totally open minded to every idea that floats your way. We need to avoid ideas whose foundation is not based in the scripture. One idea to avoid is that everybody is going to heaven. Another idea is that there is one God in heaven but he goes by different names in different cultures. This is part of the new age movement, and it nullifies what Jesus said about himself. He said, "I am the way, the truth and the life. NO MAN comes to the Father but by me." Paul also warns us to be careful not to be thrown around by every wind of doctrine that comes our way.

I think we should avoid discussion about baptisms and procedural differences. People have strong feelings about being sprinkled or dunked when being baptized. Can you imagine Saint Peter standing at the gates as you arrive shaking his head, "You laid your life down completely for the Lord except you were baptized the wrong way. I am sorry you can't come in." Doesn't that sound crazy to you? We have to realize that God is more interested in the heart than the process we follow.

I encourage you to talk to people about their religious beliefs. It can be a very rewarding and enlightening discussion. Remember it is just as important to listen to the other people's beliefs as it is expressing your own. When you share with someone outside the faith, share your personal experiences because they are more powerful than doctrines. When you share your faith with someone, allow the Holy Spirit to touch that person's heart. After all, it's His job to bring people to salvation.

Remember, listen to other's beliefs. You can learn a lot from them. Share your own beliefs, but don't cram them down someone's throat. Keep in mind it's OK to disagree with someone about what they believe. When you disagree, remember to do it in the love of the Lord. Finally, when your time of sharing comes to an end, always strive to encourage and build one another up. When you share with that in mind, you will honor the Lord.

Father, help us to share our faith with others.
Give us the words to speak, words of love and encouragement.
Jesus, let your light shine through us.
We submit to sharing with others in your way, through love.
Holy Spirit, we ask that you fill us anew
with the power of Pentecost.
Father, Son and Holy Spirit, we ask that you will lead us
into your green pastures
and down your narrow paths.
As you lead us, feed us and give us cool water to drink,
help us to remember to share those things
with the hungry & the thirsty
all around us.
Amen.

Sex, Condoms and Schools

What do sex, condoms and schools have in common? These three have more in in common than the average Christian realizes. Schools are being forced into a place where we must educate our youth about sex. Parents are failing to teach their children about sex, and now society is expecting educators to pick up the slack.

As an educator, my initial reaction is frustration with society. It tells me I must talk about sex, especially "safe sex", but heaven forbid I should mention the Bible or God in the classroom. If I tell the students premarital sex (called fornication) is wrong, parents are up in arms. It seems that all many parents want us to teach is "safe sex." The amazing thing is that doctors, the professionals, keep telling us that the only safe sex is abstinence.

Let me back up and separate several issues. First of all, I do not object to instructing the students about human reproduction. I do, however, believe that we should use BOTH the clinical and the slang terms so the students will understand. I also believe that we should instruct the students that sex is more than a physical union of two people, it is also an emotional union. (I understand that teaching them it is a spiritual union would be out of bounds for the public schools.) All of this I can accept as a part of the public school's responsibility to society.

My problem with sex education comes down to the condom. About 65% of the adults in our society want me as an educator to walk into my classroom and tell the kids that condoms are necessary for "safe sex". (According to a Charlotte Observer Poll) My problem is twofold. One, I don't believe we as educators should encourage sex when I believe sex before marriage is wrong biblically. Two, doctors keep screaming to deaf ears that condoms are not completely safe. We know statistically that about one in six condoms will break, leak or fall off. Do you want your child to be the victim of that one in six chance?

If the public schools become condom distributers, don't you think that will encourage students to experiment? If students are encouraged to experiment the chances of spreading AIDS, sexually transmitted diseases and teenage pregnancy will go through the roof. There is always proof that in schools where condoms have been distributed teenage pregnancy and sexually transmitted diseases have increased dramatically. Researchers have also discovered that several venereal diseases can go right through a condom. In some areas of the country, these diseases are almost reaching epidemic proportions.

Imagine with me, if you will, that you have a son who received a condom from school. Then, as logic would have it, he decides to use it with his girlfriend. Let's assume he has not had sex before because he was afraid of disease and getting a girl pregnant. Now he has the condom which, according to his teachers at school, will allow him to have "safe sex." Just think, sex with no consequences. What teenager wouldn't be tempted by that?

Everything goes as planned; they have sex. It's wonderful. Then he goes to take the condom off and discovers it leaked. He doesn't tell her and hopes everything will be alright. Several weeks later she ends up sick as a dog. She goes to the doctor, and surprise, she is pregnant. Then the doctor says in a low voice you are also HIV positive. She was not a virgin when she slept with your son. Your son goes to be tested, and he comes up HIV positive as well.

I know this story is a little farfetched, but who's responsibility was it that your son got HIV? Was it the girl's fault? Was it your fault as a parent? Could it be the school's fault for telling your son about "safe sex?" And how safe was "safe sex" for your son and his girlfriend? What about the child they created while having "safe sex?" Imagine if the child is born HIV positive. What kind of life will that child have? Did these two young people have, as their teachers taught them, "safe sex?"

Let me conclude by saying I know that there are many parents who do not want us teaching "safe sex" to their children. I appreciate those values. I also know the reality that young people aren't going to stop thinking or wanting to have sex. But I do not think we, as responsible adults, can stand in front of them and tell them this is the way to "safe sex" when we know it is a LIE. The solution is much more complex. Do I think we should teach the youth about contraceptives? After teaching school for ten years and seeing so many students with babies or planning on having them I am relatively certain we should. BUT ... NO contraceptive should be promoted or especially given to students as the solution. There is no such thing as "safe sex." That's a fact they should be told.

I believe it is the parent's responsibility to talk to their children and share their values with them concerning sex. I also believe we as teachers should be able to share with our students the importance of abstinence. There are many young people who sit on the fence of indecision. If their teachers could just give them a push in the RIGHT direction they might just abstain. I also believe that instruction on abstinence would be looked upon much more favorably by our Heavenly Father.

I encourage you, if you have children, to talk openly and honestly about sex with your children. It may be embarrassing, but the risks of their sexual activity are much greater than a little embarrassment. I believe if parents openly and honestly answer their children's questions, it will help remove the mystery and have a significant impact. Take time to explain what you believe is acceptable and unacceptable behavior in dating relationships. Pray for them and with them for guidance. If you do, I believe that God can do a miracle and keep them pure.

How can a young man (or woman) keep his way pure?
By living according to your Word.
Psalms 119:9

An Interview with Rossella Zini

Rossella was a foreign exchange student that took my class. What a privilege to teach such a bright individual. I interviewed Rossella for the Stanly News & Press. My article was too long and I was told to go back and edit it. Things got busy and I never got the chance to finish it. I have always felt bad about that. Here is the interview with Rossella that never made it to the press.

Rossella Zini is a student in one of my marketing classes. She impressed me as an intelligent person right from the beginning. On the third day of school for the students, I saw her sitting on a bench in the student lounge. There were several students around Rossella horse playing and talking, but Rossella was sitting there studying. That impressed me more than you can imagine.

Rossella comes from a family of four. Her older sister was recently married, and Rossella is hoping for a niece or nephew. Her mother works at home sewing for the local textile industry. Her father is a manager of a farm machine manufacturing company. Rossella has adopted Sid and Mitzie Lanier of New London as her house parents while she is living in the United States.

Rossella's home is in the northern part of Italy, about two hours from Milan. She says that the houses in Italy are smaller and closer together. If a neighbor coughs, you bless them through the wall. She says if someone has a fight with their spouse the whole neighborhood hears it.

We spent most of our interview talking about school. Her first statement was school is much easier in the United States. In Italy the students are assigned much more independent reading and homework. Rossella says she understands why more homework isn't assigned and done, because most of the students have part-time jobs. Being the Marketing teacher who encourages students to have part-time jobs as part of their education, that bothers me. I believe that working ought to be a part of one's education. The problem is student's priorities are wrong. Instead of school being the most important thing in their lives, their job becomes the most important so they can pay for their new cars.

Students in Italy attend school five hours a day, six days a week. Then they must study four or five hours a night to prepare for classes the next day. If we started to assign four or five hours of homework a night, parents would be in an uproar. Why? Easy. Their children need to be going to club meetings, sports activities and church meetings. They do not have time to do that much homework. Where is our priority? In our own defense, Rossella says that many students in Italy suffer from stress and anxiety. There ought to be a balance somewhere.

In America, we talk about high expectations for students; in Italy they live it. Rossella takes thirteen classes which meet at different times during the week, similar to a collage schedule. Classes begin at eight in the morning and the students go home at one o'clock. Last year she took three languages. Her English teacher at North Stanly says her skills in English are better than many of her classmates. She had three social studies classes, two business classes, a financial math and an economics class. Rossella told me that she wasted two hours a week in PE. I was also glad to hear that she had a required religious instruction class. Wow, what a schedule!

In each class she would have both oral and written exams. The oral exams occurred without warning. The typical class would begin with oral exams that lasted about half the period. The last half of the period the teacher would lecture and gives notes "very fast" with little or no repeating. Rossella said you learn to write quickly. Just imagine five classes with that kind of intensity. She said you are tired when you get home, but you have to eat (no school lunches) and begin studying for the next day.

There are two other interesting things she told me about education in Italy. Should you fail a course, you would have to study independently (ie. no summer school) and prepare for an oral and written exam in the fall. If you flunk the exams then you would repeat your entire schedule from the previous year. You can do this for a maximum of three courses in one year. That sounds tough to me, but it also puts the responsibility where it belongs, on the student. Another difference about education in Italy is that the students have five years of high school instead of four. One other interesting part is that students are tracked according to career choices.

I asked Rossella how she got around in Italy. She said that public transportation was excellent. In fact, she rides a public bus to and from school. There are no public school buses. I am sure some people in our school systems would like that idea. At the age of fourteen you are eligible for a license that allows you to ride a moped. Then at age sixteen you can get your motorcycle license. Finally, at eighteen you are eligible for your driver's license.

We talked about food, and, surprise, she likes Italian. Since being in America she has learned to like Mexican food. She loves for her food to be hot and spicy. She is shocked by the amount of french fries, burgers and sodas we consume. She tries to avoid them because they are fattening. She prefers chicken and white meat, but she absolutely loves fruits and vegetables. She likes water, iced tea and of course, cappuccino to drink.

I asked her if drinking was a problem in Italy. She said that anyone can buy wine and that it was a problem among the youth. On many week ends, four or five die in alcohol related incidents. It's a tragedy that the country is trying to deal with.

Finally, I asked her what she did for fun. She said besides the typical going out to eat and movie that most young people go to the disco or the local pub. The disco plays the same types of music that is popular in America. It is open Sunday afternoon for teenagers. Saturday nights and Sunday nights people in their 20's and 30's go. During the week, they have 50's or 60's night and country music nights. She says they play the music loud, and people dance the night away. At the pubs the quieter atmosphere allows you to talk with your friends.

I asked Rossella if she had any general thoughts about America. She said our lifestyle is much more relaxed. We are much more casual in church where they are much more formal. She says our retail business people are much kinder here. In Italy, if you do not buy from a shop they may be mad at you and cuss at you. They certainly would not say, "Thank-you and come back."

Rossella has already noticed our preoccupation with sex. She sees a problem with teenage pregnancy. She was shocked to learn that some of her classmates have babies. She said that young girls are having babies without knowing the meaning. They are bringing another life into this world and that there is a responsibility that goes along with that. She says that high school students should be boyfriend and girlfriend. They should be flirting and having fun. They are not ready for the responsibility of a baby. She admires them for being brave enough to keep the baby. In Italy kids wait longer to have sex. If they do get pregnant they either get married or they may abort the child.

So there you have it, Rossella's look at America compared to Italy. There are some good things and some bad things about each country. I guess there isn't any place that is perfect on earth. She says Americans look at life different than Italians. Is one better than another? Maybe being better isn't what is important. What we need to concentrate on is learning about each other and finding the things we have in common. This will draw us closer and make us real to each other. Once we have become real, then maybe we will learn to love and accept each other. Wouldn't that be a miracle?

Would I like to visit Italy someday? After meeting and getting to know Rossella, I think I would. I would like to visit some schools, meet the people, and taste some real Italian food. If you get the chance to meet and talk to Rossella while she is here, do it. I guarantee you you'll be impressed. Rossella, good luck in America this year. I hope you get to see this beautiful country and meet some of its interesting people. I also hope you will come to love this land as much as I do.

Michael Jordan

Koresh

MURDER

$

Discrimination

Death Penalty

Women

Flooding

Leaders

I Wanta Be Like ....

*I wrote this when Michael Jordon announced his
retirement from basketball.*

**Be imitators of God, therefore, as dearly loved children and
live a life of love, just as Christ loved us and gave himself
up for us as a fragrant offering and sacrifice to God.**
Ephesians 5:1 & 2

"I wanna be like Mike!" I am sure beyond a shadow of a doubt
that you know who I am talking about. I want to be like Michael
Jordon. We are both the same age, 30. The biggest difference
between Michael Jordon and Doug Creamer is that Michael is
retiring. I guess Michael is making a touch more than I am as a
school teacher. Even in retirement he will make more in one month
than I will in a number of years, maybe my whole life.

Setting aside the large sum of money, I would still like to be
like Mike. If for no other reason than I would beat the pants off my
older brother in a game of one-on-one. I bet my dad would like it if
I could be like Mike. He is a big sports fan; I bet he would eat it up
if I were a sports star.

Michael is sort of a modern day hero, something we are truly
lacking in our society. He has a good reputation and a solid
character. He has earned the right to be called great at basketball
because he has worked hard at it. When he goes out on the court he
gives it his best effort.

People today are looking for the easy way to the good life.
They want to win the big lottery and live on easy street. People
forget the words of Christ in Matt. 7:13 & 14, "For wide is the road
and easy is the path that leads to destruction, and many enter
through it. (The easy path!) But small is the gate and narrow is the
road that leads to life and only a few find it." Christ describes a
difficult and hard to find road to success.

Successful people like Michael also experience failures.
Failures must be overcome to build strength and character. Michael

lived through his fair share of failures. He was demoted his sophomore year from the varsity to the JV squad and told he wasn't going to be successful in basketball. When he graduated from high school he wanted to attend NC State but was rejected. After three years of college ball he decided to skip senior year to go to professionals. Some people thought that would be the end of Michael Jordon. Even the Chicago Bulls manager said that Michael would never make the difference for his team. No matter what people said or did Michael pressed on toward his goal. I find that inspirational.

True success in the body of Christ is not measured in dollars or cents or even by material possessions. True success is found in obedience. If you are called to be a trash collector and you do it in such a way that the love of God flows through your life, I believe God sees that as successful. Many people in the world would not agree, but I would rather be considered a success in God's eyes. I believe the true fruit of success is the fruit of the spirit; love, joy, peace, patience, kindness, goodness, faithfulness, gentleness and self-control.

Does this mean that I think Michael Jordon is not successful? NO! I believe that Michael is a Christian and leading a devoted life. Maybe the Lord led him on this path so he could be an inspiration to this generation. He has not led an easy life. The pressures and the temptations on someone in his position have got to be difficult. Has he lived the straight in narrow? Certainly not. Remember that all have sinned and fallen short of the glory of God. We all need the love and forgiveness of God to get into heaven. But has Michael found the narrow gate into heaven? I don't know, but I sure hope so! Wouldn't it be great to shoot some hoops with Michael Jordon in heaven?

Do I really want to be like Mike? Well maybe. But maybe I would rather be like Peter, Paul, King David, Daniel, John, Luke, Moses, or even Father Abraham. Actually, I think I would rather be like Doug Creamer. Now, if I could just get Doug Creamer to be more like ... Christ!!!

DISCRIMINATION

I do not like the use of the word discrimination in our society right now. It seems to me that whenever anybody feels they will not win their case based on its own merits, they yell, DISCRIMINATION. That one word evokes a whole lot of emotion. Most people try not to discriminate. This is not to say that discrimination is based on age, income, race, sex or religion does not occur, I KNOW it does.

Take the OJ Simpson case, for example. There are some people who think OJ is being discriminated against. I will be the first to say that if he is innocent, I hope OJ is found innocent. We have to remember he was arrested because the evidence points in his direction. What I do not understand is why some people believe that OJ is being accused of the crime purely because of his skin color. That is totally absurd.

We all know of cases where discrimination has occurred. Discrimination in any of its forms is wrong, period. I believe the Lord abhors it and he will deal with it harshly in the last judgement. I do not want to be standing behind the people who have discriminated during the last judgement.

With all this in mind let me share with you two news stories that I found in the *Charlotte Observer* and my concern about them. The first involves the Equal Employment Opportunity Commission (EEOC) and the second a small child in the public school system.

The EEOC, with all its intelligence, wants to make it illegal to wear Christian symbols (like crosses, pendants, earrings etc.) to work. They also want it to be illegal to read the Bible during your breaks on the job. They would consider this religious harassment. I don't know if this bothers you or not, but it bothers me. Who are they to say what I read or don't read in my free time? If this were passed, I would probably be arrested because I KNOW I have, and WILL continue to break that kind of law.

If you would like to do something about this issue, you could write. Tony Gallegos, EEOC, 10th floor, 1801 L ST. NW, Washington, D.C. 20507. I don't think I would want to work for anyone who was so closed minded that he or she would enforce such a law. What about my rights and liberties as an American Christian; don't they count in the scheme of things?

The other case involves the public schools. A teacher announced to her students that it was free reading time. They were all allowed to read anything they wanted. A student reached into her book bag and pulled out her Bible. A neighboring student asked if she could read with the first little girl. They were reading quietly together when the teacher came to check on them.

When the teacher discovered that they were reading the Bible, she instructed the little girl who brought the book to NEVER bring it to school again. She told her to put it away. Then the teacher gave the child a book full of demonic characters, witches, witchcraft and magic spells. The little girl told her parents about the situation and her parents are now suing the school system.

That bothers me! The child was told she could read whatever she desired. She chose to read the Bible. Now what in blazes is the matter with that? The Bible is full of values and good things for kids, besides the fact it's THE source of life. If the child was reading about Buddha, I would defend her right to do that too. It was a "free reading time."

These issues should stir you up. What should you do about them? First, pray for God's wisdom. Then follow his instructions. For some you may feel the need to pray for our children. Others of you may be lead to get involved with your child's education. Still others may be lead to write letters to the EEOC. Again, the main thing to do is pray for God's direction and then ... do it! (PS: Whatever you do be polite and respectful. God would NOT want you to be rude.)

Who was David Koresh?

I originally wrote this column in the future tense. However, before the paper went to press, the Branch Davidians Compound burned to the ground.
I rewrote the column in the form you see here.
David Koresh was the leader of the Branch Davidian Compound.

Was David Koresh Jesus Christ? Was David the anti-Christ, Satan or the beast? If David was Jesus, why didn't the church recognize him? If David was not Jesus, then what do we need to learn from the situation in Waco, Texas?

Let's start with the easiest one, was David, Jesus? Absolutely not! Did I say that clearly enough? David was positively, no question about it, you can bet your bottom dollar that he was NOT Jesus. One simple clue; Jesus is not coming back with guns. However, we do need to keep in mind that when Jesus does come back there will be a huge war, but he will not fight with guns. Also, when Jesus comes back it will signal the end of the world the way we know it.

So what was David? Is it possible that he was Satan in the flesh? No, I do not believe he was the anti-christ. The anti-christ will be a great world leader, something in the mold of a Hitler. David Koresh was one of the many false prophets that Jesus foretold would come at the end of the age. Was he a demon possessed man? Quite possible, or maybe he was just plain out of his head. One thing for sure, he will go down in the history books as a Jim Jones of the nineties. You can also be sure there are plenty more out there that are self-deceived just like David.

What should our reaction be to a cult leader like David Koresh? I think we should pray for their followers and the little children. These are the real victims in any cult. Imagine the mental and emotional scars people will have if they are lucky enough to escape from a cult. The people will probably never come to know the true savior. So I think our reaction should also include evangelism. This is the perfect opportunity to share the gospel and the love of God with the people around you.

Where will Jesus make his appearance? Will it be in the U.S.? To steal an expression from our youth, NOT! Jesus will make his appearance in Israel. Remember Jesus was a Jew. He also focused most of his ministry on the Jewish people. Scripture promises that a remnant of Jews will turn to the Lord before he returns. The Jewish people, as I have said before, are God's chosen people. Scripture also points out that He will return riding on the clouds. Most Bible scholars believe that he will "touch down" on the Mount of Olives, just outside Jerusalem.

What does all this say about the times in which we are living? Jesus's first statement in Matt. 24 is watch out that no one deceives you. Jesus warns that there will be many like David Koresh. Jesus said these are the first signs of the end of this age. Don't panic, I don't believe Jesus's return is eminent, but I do think we need to watch the signs of our times. I also think the key to keep in mind is what Jesus said in Matt. 24:36 "No one knows the day or the hour (of Jesus's return), not even the angels in heaven, nor the Son, but ONLY the Father."

So again, what does all this mean to us? What should we do? I think we need to live our everyday lives in a way that pleases the Lord. This means we need to love our neighbor as we love ourselves (and as God loves us). This means that we should be the salt of the earth, the preservative to our dying and decaying world. We should be a lighthouse, a beacon, to a dark and lost world. We should be the fragrance of a loving God. We should carry the bread and the new wine to a starving and thirsty land. We should be men and women of prayer, intercessors, remembering that the prayer of a righteous man or woman is powerful and effective. (James 5:16)

I would also like to encourage you to pray for the cult members' families. There must be a bunch of questions and a lot of pain and bitterness. Pray that the Lord will draw near to them and comfort them and strengthen their faith. Also brace yourself because there will be more false prophets like David Koresh in the future. I encourage you to get to know your savior intimately so you will not be deceived when these men come. May God's peace and love rest upon you.

Lord, help us to listen only for your voice.
Forgive us when we look to someone else for the
answers to life's questions.
Help us Lord, to be loyal sheep who follow you, our shepherd.
And Father, when we wonder from your side,
please come after us like a shepherd
looking for the lost sheep.
And when you find us,
return us to your side, where we belong.
Father, we love you!
Thank you for sending us the Good Shepherd,
Jesus Christ, our Lord.
Amen.

Is It Murder?

*Do two wrongs make a right? Didn't the Lord say,
"Vengeance is mine?" When should we stand up
against the evils in our society and how?*

I don't know how many of you heard the news from Friday, July 29, 1994. There was a doctor, John Britton, and a volunteer, James Barrett, murdered in cold blood outside the doctor's clinic in Pensacola, Florida. The doctor was an abortionist. The murderer was Paul Hill, a former Presbyterian minister, who considered the murders justifiable homicide.

I cannot believe that a minister would murder someone in cold blood and think that God would consider it a great accomplishment. In my mind, this minister has done something far worse than the abortion doctor ever did. He has also hurt the cause of the Pro-Life organizations. These types of tactics are wrong, totally ungodly and unbiblical. Abortion is wrong and it is also MURDER. We as Christians must stand up and proclaim that abortion is ungodly.

At the national prayer breakfast this year Mother Teresa warned America. She spoke candidly, vividly and directly against America's greatest sin, abortion. The Pope has spoken to President Clinton on at least two occasions that America must repent of this travesty. Both indicated that if America did not repent of these sins they felt the Lord's hand of grace would be removed from America. I don't know how you feel about that, but it scares the heck out of me.

One thing that interested me about these warnings was that there was little press coverage or publicity. Isn't this the kind of thing the press would like to blow up? I can imagine the headlines now, "Spiritual leaders warn the President and the nation to repent!" The reason we needed to repent would be buried somewhere on page four. If they had spoken about education or violence in our society their comments would have made the front pages of all the major papers. When it comes to abortion as sin the issue so sharply divides the nation that the newspapers don't want to touch it.

We as Christians need to take our stand on the issue, but what should we do? I know some things we shouldn't do. First, murdering an abortion doctor is not the answer. I also disagree with yelling at people who enter the clinics. Telling them they are murders or that they are going to hell is not going to help the situation or them.

There are some things that would be helpful. First, we must remember that, "our struggle is not against flesh and blood, but against the rulers, against the authorities, against the powers of this dark world and against the spiritual forces of evil in the heavenly realms." (Eph. 6:12) So we must begin out battle on our knees in prayer. You know, the most effective thing that could be done outside an abortion clinic is a group of people QUIETLY praying. They should not say a word to those entering, but they should pray hard for their salvation. Now that would be a good beginning.

Another helpful thing would be financially supporting a Crisis Pregnancy Clinic (CPC). These pro-life clinics provide women counseling during a dark and difficult time in their lives. There are many of these around that are so underfunded that even a small monthly gift could keep these organizations alive. You could take some training and become a CPC counselor. There is a major shortage of them because there is usually no pay. Another way you could help is by opening the doors of your heart and home to a woman who is having a crisis pregnancy. Many young girls, particularly those under the age of 18, are told to abort it or move out by their parents. If they decide to keep the baby they have nowhere to go. Imagine the opportunity you might have to witness to the scared young adult and her child.

There are also some other basic needs such as clothing, baby food and used baby furniture that would help these clinics meet the needs of new mothers. Again, your gift of money might help save one baby's life.

I hope you get the idea that God has plenty of ways you can help the Pro Life cause. I encourage you to find out how you can be involved in a positive way on this important issue! God can use you, if you are available.

Jesse

I can do everything through Him (Jesus Christ)
who gives me strength.
Philippians 4:13

I had the privilege of attending a men's breakfast at church. I really enjoy getting together with the other men, but I do not like getting up so early on a Saturday morning. The food is usually good and there is always a speaker.

The speaker at this breakfast was very good. He stood up and shared his testimony. The stories he told about himself made you want to bust out laughing one minute and cry the next. The testimony was so powerful that I thought it would be good to share it with you.

When Jesse, the speaker, was born there was not a lot of rejoicing. Jesse's mother had a difficult time delivering him. The doctor had to use the forceps to help get him out. In the process the doctor damaged Jesse's cerebellum which controls the motor skills. The doctor also damaged the nerve that controls the mouth and speech. Jesse's parents were told that Jesse would never walk or talk.

Jesse's parents were determined to prove the doctors wrong. They worked with him every day trying to get him to walk. Sometimes they would literally drag him up and down a long hall until he learned to walk. Although he made grunts and noises louder than most children, his parents worked with him constantly to help him overcome his speech impediments.

When he reached the age of five his parents wanted to enroll him in public school. Jesse is about sixty now, and when he was five schools were not equipped for handicapped children. His determined parents told the school system they better get equipped.

The first day of school was a disaster. Children can be terrible to others who are less fortunate than themselves. They lived up to their reputation with Jesse. After four days he dropped out. He tried re-enrolling the next fall and received the same treatment. He dropped out for the second time. The next fall he enrolled for his third attempt at school. Again, the children laughed at him because he was different. This time instead of crying, he turned around and laughed with them. Jesse said that somehow God supernaturally put a sense of humor in him about his condition. His perspective changed and he was able to laugh with the other children.

Jesse was the high school team's water boy and he graduated with high honors. He was voted the most friendly and most likely to succeed. He went on to college and studied to be a minister. This is really ironic because Jesse still speaks with a speech impediment.

There were two scriptural stories that Jesse drew upon to share his testimony. The first was the calling of Moses to go free the Israelites from Egypt. Moses complained that he could not speak, so how could he go and speak to Pharaoh. Jesse complained to God in the same way, how could he be a preacher when people have a difficult time understanding him. If you ever hear Jesse speak you will understand the miracle that God does to help him speak and to help you understand.

The other story he drew upon was the little boy in the feeding of the five thousand. The little boy offered the give his five loaves and two fish and Jesus multiplied it to feed the five thousand. Jesse asked us if we had given our five loaves and two fishes or our talents and abilities to God. If we do, then God can multiply them and reach a world of people around us.

I was personally challenged by all that Jesse said. I noticed that Jesse was a man who faced more difficulties every day than I face in a week, yet he was not complaining or blaming anybody. He had the love, joy and the peace of Jesus in his heart. He knows he has a redeemer and a loving father waiting for his arrival in heaven.

I encourage you to offer your gifts and abilities to God. He may challenge you to use them in ways that you believe are impossible for you to do. Don't worry; they are impossible for you to do. But with God working through you all things are possible. I encourage you to reach out and accomplish that thing that God has been stirring in your heart and spirit to do. I bet He'll meet you and help you if you do.

Father, help us to be thankful
for the good things you give us.
Lord, help us to be faithful
with the gifts and talents you give us.
Lord, help us to give our talents
in service to your kingdom.
Help us Father, to reach out and touch
the people who are on your heart.
Thank you, Lord.
Amen.

God's Ways Are Higher

Then I heard the Voice of the Lord saying,
"Whom shall I send? And who will go for us?"
And I said, "Here I am Lord. Send me."
Isaiah 6:8

I went to a men's breakfast a few Saturday's ago. The gentlemen who spoke had been diagnosed with throat cancer. He had an operation where they removed the cancer and some surrounding lymph nodes from his throat. It seemed like it required a great deal of effort for him to talk. His story touched my heart and I hope it touches yours.

Billy said he received the grave news one afternoon. He drove home and sat quietly in his dining room waiting for his wife to come home. Two significant things occurred while he was waiting. The first thing he did was pray and commit the entire situation to the Lord's hands. Bill was a Christian and he was not afraid to die. The second thing that happened was that he felt the Lord telling him to read Isaiah 55 and that the Lord was in control of the situation.

Bill opened his Bible and read Isaiah 55 and the verse that stuck out to him was verse 8, "For my thoughts are not your thoughts, neither are my ways your ways." The next few weeks were bleak as family and doctors gave him little hope of surviving.

A short time later a women he knew called and asked him if he would be willing to go to Mexico for treatment. Since he did not feel good about the radical surgery that the doctors recommended, he was open to going to Mexico. He prayed about it and felt the Lord was telling him to go. After he made the decision to go the Lord provided all the finances, a story within itself.

Bill said there were patients from all over the world at the hospital. They all had cancer and they all had stories about how they had been led by the Lord to come to this hospital in Mexico. This amazed Bill.

One evening, after he had been there for about a month, the

Lord spoke to him as he was returning to his room for the evening. The Lord told him to go and pray with this woman named Mary from England. He decided to get on the elevator and not listen. The Lord did not allow the elevator to move no matter how many buttons he pushed. When the doors on the elevator reopened on the same floor he quickly exited and became obedient.

He knocked on Mary's door. When she answered he introduced himself and asked if he could come in and pray. She seemed really surprised but agreed. They shared their cancer stories and prayed together. That was a Friday night.

The next night the Lord told him to go and pray with her again. This time he went directly to her room. When he walked into her room he noticed pictures of Buddha, Gandhi and Jesus. He used the opportunity to share the gospel with the woman. After sharing with her, they prayed. He was just about to lead her through the sinner's prayer when his throat closed up on him. He could not breathe; in fact, the doctors had to put him on respirators.

Later that evening as he began to calm down in his room the Lord spoke to him again. Go home. That was all he heard. He complained to the Lord about the fact that the cancer was not healed. Then he felt the Lord remind him of the verse, "For my thoughts are not your thoughts, neither are your ways my ways." So he came home and received the radical surgery that the doctors recommended before he went to Mexico.

Sometime later while he was recovering from his surgery the phone rang. It was a woman he had met in the hospital in Mexico who lived in New York. They talked for a while and just before the woman hung up she said, "Oh by the way, you remember Mary (the woman he prayed with), she gave her life to the Lord the Sunday after you left."

Isn't that amazing! God brought a man from High Point North Carolina and a woman from England together in Mexico so she could hear the word of the Lord and commit her life to Christ. God's ways truly are higher than our ways. He spares no expense to call us into His kingdom.

God's got it all in control

B J Thomas was one of the first Christian music artists I liked. I liked the stories in his songs and I liked his style. He helped me make the switch from rock music to contemporary Christian music. One of my favorite songs that he sang was, "He's got it all in control." It helped me during a time when my life was changing. The refrain to the song goes, "He's got it all in control. God's got it all in control. He's put that reassurance way down in my soul. He's got it all in control."

I have watched with a great deal of interest the story of the comets hitting Jupiter. I bet if OJ Simpson wasn't monopolizing our news, we would have gotten much more on the comets. The collision of the comets with Jupiter had an unbelievable effect. Don't miss understand me, it hasn't pushed Jupiter off its path or anything. It's the size of the explosion on impact that is so unbelievable to me.

There has been much speculation about what would happen if such a comet were to hit the earth. I wonder if it could happen? I recently read in the paper that a big comet missed the earth by six hours. I guess anything is possible. But I really don't believe anything like that will ever occur because God has a vested interest here on earth, his children. We have to remember that no matter how bad things may look at times, God is still in control. I trust that the scripture says, "His eye is on the sparrow and I know he watches me." I don't think he is going to allow the earth to be destroyed by a comet. We have to remember that he has plans for us.

I know one of my neighbors would be in a good place to question God's sovereign control. This family had more happen to it in the last year than any family deserves. The wife has had two major operations in the last year. The husband had one major operation in the past year. The wife lost two very close family members this year and the husband lost one very close family member this year. Yesterday, I heard the wife is scheduled to go have some "tests" done. I think there is room in their lives to question God about their situation. The encouraging news is that the husband knows that God is in control. He said he and his family could "feel" the prayers of their friends and neighbors.

When things are going along well for us we know God is in control. However, when things go crazy and some terrible and tough things begin to occur to us we immediately question whether God is in control. Look back on your own life, think back on those terrible tough times, was God in control? I bet looking back on those situations you can see the hand of the Lord. You can see where God was carrying you through those difficult times.

I believe that God allows these difficult things to occur to illustrate to us that "yes, I will be with you." God wants us to know we can trust him completely especially during those difficult times. God is there as a comforting friend to listen to us and allow us to cry on his shoulder.

Another reason God allows difficult times is that most of us turn to prayer for comfort. That's what God wants. He wants fellowship with his children. When we are in the "good times" we often forget God and forget to pray. I believe that God misses us and wants our fellowship so bad that he will allow bad things in our lives to drive us back to him.

Don't twist what I am saying around. When bad things happen to people it is not a direct cause of sin or the fact they aren't praying regularly. Everybody has tough times, even those who keep regular quiet times. It really bothers me when people say, "Something bad happened to that person. I wonder what they did to deserve that." This gives God a bad image and one that I believe is not true.

The bottom line to all this is that God is in control. He is in control of the difficult times and the good times too. God deeply desires to give us good things in our lives. But it is during those difficult and dry times that we have to remind ourselves that God does love us and that he is in total control. May God bless you and keep you in both the good and the bad times.

Could the Flooding be a Message From Above?

No one knows about that day or hour,
not even the angels in heaven,
nor the Son, but only the Father.
As it was in the days of Noah,
so it will be at the coming
of the Son of Man.
Matthew 24:36 & 37

Anyone who has read the newspaper or listened to the news knows about the flooding going on in and around the Mississippi River. I talked to a friend who has family up in that area of the country and he said that dams and levees are at capacity or breaking. It seems amazing to me as I watch the weather maps on the evening news how the storms keep coming. They are flooded and we are parched.

It seems to me that there have been many natural disasters occurring around the world in the last year. Japan just got rocked by a large earthquake. Hurricane Calvin hit Mexico. Hurricane Andrew crushed Florida and Texas. The Hawaiian Islands were hit by a powerful hurricane. There was the big snow storm that hit the East Coast this past winter. I remember reading this past winter that Israel was getting more snow than they had received in years.

Is it possible that these are signs of the end of the world? You know Jesus said that no one knows when the end of the world will occur. He said that even he didn't know. But Jesus taught that we could know the signs of the end just like we know the signs of the changes in the seasons.

Jesus was asked in Matthew 24, what are the signs of the end times? The first thing he said was there will be wars and rumors of wars. I read recently that there are about 150 areas of civil unrest (wars) in the world. Jesus also said that famines and earthquakes would occur around the world. Greensboro, North Carolina had a small earthquake the other day as well as the big one in Japan. I think California has little ones every day. When it comes to places suffering from famines my mind travels to places like Somalia, Romania, Albania and Russia.

Jesus said that Christians will be hated and persecutes. Christians in America are relatively free of persecution except when it comes to wanting prayer in school and Right to Life rallies. In other places around the world, Christians are not so lucky. Take the Middle East, for example, where the Muslim and Islamic religions are strong. If you proclaim your Christian faith openly over there, the Muslims have a duty to kill you. They persecute Jews and Christians equally. As a side note, you should know that the Muslim religion is the fastest growing religion in America. So is persecution possible in America? I would say, it is on the horizon.

Jesus also teaches that many false prophets will appear near the end to deceive people. Most people in America will agree that David Koresh and Jim Jones were false prophets. But many people are having trouble seeing the more subtle false prophets. There are people teaching that there is only one god. They say that people all around the world are worshipping the same god, just calling him by a different name. This is a New Age philosophy. This contradicts what the Bible and Jesus teach. Jesus said, "I am the way the truth and the life. No one comes to the Father except through me." (John 14:6) So maybe there are a lot of false prophet around.

Jesus pointed out that there will be an increase in wickedness. Wickedness means morally very bad, fierce and vicious behavior. Take one glance at the front of this paper or turn on any of the local news stations and I am convinced you will hear of or see wicked behavior. In some of the major cities there are more murders than can be reported.

Jesus said that there would also be an increase in pestilence. My Webster Dictionary says that is an infectious epidemic disease that is devastating. As I read this, I thought about Aids.

One of the last things Jesus says will occur is that the gospel will go out to all nations before the end will come. Organizations like Wycliffe Bible Translators and the Gideon's are making progress on this goal daily.

By looking at the signs of the time, could we be approaching the last days? I don't know! However, I don't plan to be one of the scoffers. At the same time I am not going to worry about it. I plan to live every day to the best of my ability for Jesus.

I would like to encourage you to live each day for Him too. Remember that no one knows when Jesus is coming back. We do, however, know the signs of his return. The signs seem to be pointing to the fact that we must be close. I can't say it enough, prepare your heart by reading His word and praying. I encourage you to accept His love and to walk in His paths and to keep in mind that His return is coming soon. God Bless You.

The Spirit and the Bride say, "Come!"
And let him who hears say, "Come!"
and whoever wishes,
let him take the free gift
of the water of life.
He who testifies to these things says,
"Yes, I am coming soon."
Amen. Come Lord Jesus.
The grace of the Lord Jesus
be with God's people.
Amen.
Revelation 22:17, 20 & 21

Money Talks

*Suppose a man comes into your meeting wearing
a gold ring and fine clothes, and a poor man in
shabby clothes also comes in. If you show special
attention to the man wearing fine clothes and say,
"Here's a good seat for you," but say to the poor man,
"You stand there" or "Sit on the floor by my feet,"
have you not discriminated among yourselves
and become judges with evil thoughts?
James 2:2 – 4*

I was fortunate enough to have the opportunity to attend a Charlotte Hornets basketball game. The Hornets were playing the Bulls. Talk about excited, I couldn't wait. I got home early the day of the big game hoping to take a little nap, ha, that was a joke. Who could possibly sleep when they were getting ready to go see the Bulls and the Hornets play for the first time.

There was a group of six of us that rode a tour bus together. We arrived an hour and a half early. It was great because we got the chance to watch some of the players warm up. We walked down as close as the ushers would allow us. My neighbor's brother-in-law wanted to get his two teenage sons as close to the court as possible.

When he asked if they could get closer the usher said no. He politely tried to persuade her to allow his sons a closer view to take pictures. She wouldn't budge. I tried appealing to her sensitive caring side with, "Come on, they are just kids hoping to get a close up of one of the stars." She smiled. Evidently someone had tried that on her before.

I turned back to my friend and shrugged my shoulders. So he reached in his pocket and pulled out a money clip. He pulled off some money and prepared to give it to her. I decided to walk away because I thought she was going to stone wall him and embarrass us all. I turned back a minute later to see her escorting the kids to front row seats. I couldn't believe it. I walked back to my friend who was smiling from ear to ear. He simply said, "Money talks."

It's a sad fact, but money does talk. The question on my mind is does it talk in our churches? I can almost hear you saying "yes" from here. Why do we allow people who have money to influence the church?

If a new family started to attend any church and they gave a thousand dollars a month they would quickly become influential. We would make sure they had good seats and we would be willing to change things to suit them. If they thought something was important we would jump to please them.

In contrast if an average family began attending the church, they might be unnoticed because of the excitement over the rich family. The poorer family may be willing to accept things being done differently. They wouldn't threaten to hold back their money because they didn't get things their way. This family would have to fend for themselves while people gave preferential treatment to the rich family.

This is something we are warned against doing, especially in the church. God is not a respecter of money, so why are we? Can you imagine getting to the pearly gates and seeing a guy in line ahead of you getting the bad news. As he is talking with Peter you see him slip Peter some money. Then you see Peter look around and take it. He smiles and opens the door for the man. The man straightens his robe and walks through the door. Then he falls into one of those holes that the Road Runner always puts in front of Wild Coyote. As the man is falling, Peter yells, "Sorry, that stuff is no good up here!"

Money, the Bible says, is the root of all evil. With it we are able to buy anything we want for personal pleasure. We can use it to gain influence over others. We also use it to pay our bills. We pay for our cars and houses. Don't misunderstand my point; God wants to give us good things. Sometimes that involves money or some of the comforts of life. These things are not necessarily evil or bad.

The important question is, who controls your money? Do you control it and have the final say on where it goes? Or do you allow God to direct where your money gets spent? Do you use your money to help the weak, to feed the hungry and to make the less fortunate lives a little easier. If God directed you to give some money away, could you? Would you? If God is in control of your money, it is not an evil thing. In fact, everything belongs to God anyway, so why not let him direct where He wants you to spend the portion He gives you?

Money can't buy you genuine love or happiness. It can't buy your salvation. Money may talk, but not to God. I encourage you to listen to God, see what He would have you do with your money....I mean His money.

Lord, Money is a gift from you.
Help us to be faithful
with that Gift.
Teach us to spend it wisely
and show us where we need to
give to help your kingdom.
Father, we want to invest in heaven
because that is our true reward.
Amen.

Fallen Sinner

*I have a missionary friend who goes into very poor countries.
He says that the people are very hungry and poor yet they can
tell you what is going on in the OJ trial. They watch it on TV.*

*This was written shortly after OJ's arrest.
I know people have a strong feeling one way or the other
about the OJ case. Please keep in mind, my thoughts
relate to our court system and justice in eternity,
not specifically with my opinion of the OJ Simpson case.*

As anybody living in this country already knows a major hero
was arrested the other day for a double murder. I am speaking
about OJ Simpson. OJ is, according to the average American, a
superstar. He made it big in football and then made it big in
broadcasting. Now to many people's surprise he is under arrest for
the double murder of his wife and a male friend.

Over the many weeks to come there will be many articles
written about the man and this "unfortunate situation." I heard
tonight that there are several books being worked on about his life
and the events leading up to the murders. You know that there will
be movies made of these events too. I would like to focus my
article on a different point of view than the many others that have
proceeded mine and the many others that will follow.

OJ Simpson is an All-American-Hero. He played outstanding
high school, college and professional football. He made something
great out of his life, his earthly life. I was wondering about the
more important issues at hand. Is OJ a Christian? Does OJ believe
that there is a God who can be there for him at this time in his life?

Many people seemed shocked when the news broke of the
murders and that OJ might be connected. I personally wished it
wasn't true. However, the reality is that OJ, just like the rest of us,
is a sinner. When someone becomes a hero like OJ has become we
expect them to be perfect. The truth is they are sinners just like the

rest of us. We also need to avoid pointing fingers at him because all of us are capable of doing the same thing he is accused of doing. Your reaction might be that you would never do such a thing, but you don't know the circumstances.

Celebrities and athletes are not the only ones we think are "perfect." Pastors often get lumped into the group of people who are expected to be "perfect." Pastors get tired and cranky, they even get angry. In our society we don't allow them to be human.

Many pastors burn out because they don't have someone to pastor them. They need someone to listen to their problems, someone to unload on. They need our prayers. If we put our pastors up on pedestals, they will fall off, or the Lord will push them off. We all need to remember to allow them the chance to make mistakes.

One of my concerns about the OJ case, if he is found guilty, is that he will dodge the sentence through the use of the insanity plea. I personally believe we need to change our system and stop allowing people to plead innocent by reason of insanity. The new plea should be GUILTY but insane. My feeling is; if you do the crime, you need to do the time.

Can you imagine, again supposing that OJ is guilty, him standing before Jesus Christ at the last judgement. "OJ why did you do it?" the Lord would ask. "Lord," OJ would respond, "it was society's fault. They made me into a super hero and I couldn't handle the pressure. Besides the courts found me to be innocent by reason of insanity."

"OJ," I believe the Lord would respond, "you are responsible for your actions. You claim to be the victim. I challenge you to look at your children and these two people whose lives ended early because of you. Look at the incredible pain you caused their families to face. And you have the gall to stand there and claim to be the victim. NO! You are guilty as charged!"

OJ's only hope, if he is guilty, is the same hope we all have, Jesus Christ and Him crucified. Remember we are all sinners guilty before God. We are also capable of anything including murder. Please pray for OJ and the families involved. The pain, the confusion and the questions have got to be difficult to deal with. Pray that God will release his ministering angels to comfort them.

No one knows when their lives will come to an end. I just read in the paper this week where a whole family died in a tragic car crash. There is no guarantee of tomorrow. I encourage you to personally call upon Jesus while there is still time. He wants to get to know you and He especially wants you to know Him. I pray the Lord's peace will fill your hearts as you seek to know Him better.

For it is by grace you have been saved,
through faith-
and this is not from yourselves,
it is the gift of God-
not by works,
so no one can boast.
Ephesians 2:8

Women in Leadership

There has been a huge uproar within the Church of England. What happened? The leadership within the church decided to allow women to become priests. This has caused some of the male priests to leave the Church of England.

This has caused me to ask many questions of myself and those around me. I know that we have churches here in America that are ordaining women. In fact, the church that was hit by the terrible tornado in Piedmont, Alabama recently was co-pastored by a woman. What should a woman's role be in a church? The answers vary depending on who you ask.

There are examples from scripture of women who were spiritual leaders. There is Esther who saved her people from annihilation. There is Deborah who helped lead the Army of Israel in battle. Sarah, Rachel, Ruth and Rebecca are all Godly women from the scripture. There was also Mary the mother of our Lord. There was Mary Magdalene, the first person the Lord appeared to after his death. Were these women spiritual leaders?

Do you believe that God told Joan of Arc what to do to help the French? Here is a woman who had visions from heaven and wisdom from God on how to defeat the enemy. The Catholic Church considers her a saint. Was she a spiritual leader?

Then there are some modern examples of Godly women who are leaders. The list seems impressive. Let's start with Mother Teresa. Here is a woman who has laid down her life for the poor. What about Corrie Ten-Boom? She has witnessed to millions of people about the power and love of God. Margret Thatcher is a woman who is highly regarded for her leadership skills and abilities. Think about Amy Grant, Sandi Patti and Twila Paris. Here are three women who have used their singing talents to win the lost for the Lord. Are these women spiritual leaders?

I know that there are several denominations who are ordaining women into pastoral positions. One family that I am very close to has a woman as their pastor. They say it's different but they like her. In Rowan County I know of at least two women who are pastors. One woman gave up her pastoral position because men were not comfortable with her in that position.

What should a woman's role be in the church? To be completely honest, I don't know. There are some roles that I feel women can confidently fill, but I am not sure if they should be the senior pastors of churches.

I think women make excellent counselors. I believe within the church structure women should be involved in counseling, particularly for other women. Women also make great teachers. Most of my Sunday school and public education teachers were women. There is a need for more men to be involved in teaching Sunday school, but that's another column. Women make great adult Sunday school teachers and I have even heard several women give excellent teachings in the Sunday morning service.

Scripture mentions several examples of women who were in the role of a deacon. This role involved being a caretaker of the physical building. Deacons also help to meet the people's physical needs and some spiritual needs.

The ultimate question remains, should women be pastors? Again, I confess that I do not have the answer. But, I wonder if the following scripture might shed a positive light on the question. In Acts 2:17 & 18 it says, "In those days, God says, I will pour out my spirit on all people. Your sons and daughters will prophesy .... Even on my servants, both men and women, I will pour out my spirit in those days." Does this mean that women will be pastors in the last days?

The only conclusions I can make from this quest is the following. We need to remember that God can use anybody who is a willing servant, man or woman. We need to pray and seek the Lord for what he thinks is right for us and for our individual churches. Then we need to pray for the women who are pastors and leaders, regardless of how we feel about them being in those positions. This would please the Lord. If there are any woman pastors who read this, I pray God will bless you.

I encourage you to take time today to encourage the women who are playing vital leadership roles in your church.

Sin is Not a Laughing Matter

I have always enjoyed the comics in the paper. If one of the strips is particularly funny, I will laugh out loud. Once, I was laughing so loud that a friend came to see what was so funny. He could not believe that I was laughing that hard at the comics.

There has been so much discussion among people I know concerning one particular comic strip recently. It has to do with an issue that has been hotly debated in the news lately too. The issues is homosexuality and the comic strip is, *For Better or For Worse.* In the comic strip, Michael one of the main characters, has a friend who has just admitted to being a homosexual. This open admission in the comic strip and the issue of homosexuals in the military has caused many people to discuss and to take sides on the issue.

Is homosexuality right or wrong? The truth is that it is wrong. Period. Let me support this *opinion* the only way I know how, through scripture. In the Old Testament, the cities of Sodom and Gomorrah were destroyed by God. If you will read Gen. 19:4 & 5 you will notice that men of Sodom wanted to commit homosexual acts with the angels that came to destroy the cities. There were many other sins being committed in Sodom and Gomorrah, but this is the one that caused God to want to destroy those cities.

Jesus talks about being clean and unclean in Mark 7:14-23. Jesus says that the things that make a person unclean are the things that come out of the heart. One of those items on the list is sexual immorality which includes homosexuality.

Finally, I would like to point out I Corinthians 6:9-11. In this passage of scripture Paul lists several kinds of sinful acts including homosexuality. He says that people who practice these type things will not inherit the kingdom of God. This is probably a very difficult statement for many of us, as we all probably know someone who is a homosexual.

Will there be anybody in heaven who was a homosexual? The answer can be found in I Corinthians 6:11. "And this is what some of you were." (A list that includes homosexuals) "BUT you were washed, you were sanctified, you were justified in the name of the Lord Jesus Christ and by the Spirit of our God." If someone repents for their sin, including homosexuality, they can be forgiven and given a place in heaven.

How should we as Christians deal with people who are homosexuals? For my answer, I try to imagine Jesus and how he would deal with them. I do not see Jesus carrying picket signs and yelling at the homosexuals that they better repent or they are going to hell. I also do not see Jesus patting them on the back and saying, "Come on and be a member of my church and you can keep living anyway you want."

The way I imagine Jesus treating homosexuals is the same way he dealt with sinners when he was living on the earth. He would go to them and love the person and hate the sin. Do you realize that Jesus was found with the tax collectors, prostitutes and other sinners? When he was questioned about it his answer was simple, "It is not the healthy who need a doctor, but the sick."

Don't you think this ought to be the way we treat anybody who is lost in sin? Instead of standing there condemning the person for whatever sin they are in, shouldn't we try to love them. I think we also need to lovingly and compassionately help them to see the error of their way.

Isn't that what Good Friday is all about? We ALL need to take our sin, whatever it is, to the cross of our Lord. Then, and only then, can we experience the love and forgiveness of God. Then, and only then, can we know the grace and power of our resurrected Lord on Easter morning.

God bless you and Happy Easter.

Pray for those that you know who are homosexuals.
Pray they will repent and receive God's love and forgiveness.

The Death Penalty from a Christian Perspective

I recently read in the Salisbury Post where the death penalty was given to James Campbell for the rape and murder of a twenty year old woman. The paper reported that this is the first death sentence that has been imposed in Rowan County since the death penalty was reinstated.

I believe in the death penalty. My conviction comes from my Christian faith. After reading about the death penalty in the paper, I searched the scriptures for answers to my questions about the ethics of such a conviction. I searched with an open mind willing to change my convictions. I say this because I know that anybody who does research can find things to support their point of view.

The first thing I noticed was the Ten Commandments. They say, "Thou shall not MURDER." Notice the word is not kill. There is a big difference between murdering someone and killing someone. Murder is premeditated. Killing could be driving down the road and having an accident where one of the people involved dies. If the person responsible was on drugs or alcohol, then I believe that what appears to be an accident is really murder.

During times of war, when you shoot or bomb an enemy and they die, that would be killing, not murder. Remember, David from the Old Testament was considered a mighty warrior. He was mighty in battle and the Lord was with him, especially when he killed Goliath. Also, remember when Joshua crossed the Jordan River, the first person he came in contact with was the captain of the army of the Lord. This implies a mighty warrior ready for battle, which includes killing.

I looked for a New Testament reference that would support or reject capital punishment. The first thing I stumbled across was Ananias and Sapphira. These two had sold a piece of property and kept part of the money for themselves. The problem was not keeping some money, rather lying when they said they gave it all to the disciples and to the Lord. When each of them publicly professed their lie they dropped dead in the presence of the Lord. Imagine how people would react if that happened in churches today.

Just when I thought I had come to a conclusion, I read something from two highly regarded Christian writers. Both differed in their view of capital punishment. One talked about the cost of keeping a person locked up (over $17,000 a year). He also pointed out that about 85% of those released from prison would be back. That should tell us that something is not working. He points out that back in Biblical times those who committed minor crimes were required to pay back four or five times what they had taken. For more serious crimes public whipping and capital punishment were the order.

The other author wrote something that was convicting. He said that he had a Christian friend who was scheduled to go to the electric chair. The minister said, "Love, I've discovered, leaves no room for vengeance." Ouch! This reminded me of the time that the Pharisees brought the woman caught in adultery to Jesus seeking his opinion. According to Jewish law she should have been stoned to death. His answer was that anyone who had not committed sin should be the first to throw a stone at her. This reveals the depth of the mercy and forgiveness of God for everyone.

I also thought about the criminal on the cross next to Christ. Remember he asked Christ to remember him. Christ granted that criminal eternal life right there moments before he died. Yet the criminal still had to suffer capital punishment for the crimes he had committed. So the mercy of God can be extended to the criminal while justice is served.

What are my conclusions concerning capital punishment. At this time I still favor it in some circumstances. I don't relish the thought of killing a man or woman, but remembering the victims and those left behind, it may be a fair solution. Also, it may deter others from committing horrible crimes. I do agree with the judge who, after reading the sentence to James Campbell, said, "God have mercy on his soul."

Rainbows
& Smiles

The other morning I was driving to work. I suppose that the dark cloud that was over head could have been my thoughts. There was a lot on my mind as I was driving to work. I was worried about a conference that I was planning and about my classes for that day. I was not my normal, happy self.

As I was passing Pfeiffer College and all the construction that has been going on, I noticed several cars coming from the other direction with their lights on. I knew it was not supposed to rain so I did not understand why their lights were on. As I drove farther I noticed a few drops of rain falling on my car. Finally, as I reached the Richfield stoplight a full shower was in progress. This added a new dimension to my gloom and doom.

I was glad to see the sun poke its head out as I reached New London. As I looked back at the small shower I saw some color in the sky. I was sure it was a rainbow. I nearly had an accident trying to get a view of it. When I parked my car at North Stanly I quickly got out of the car so I could see the rainbow. It had to be one of the most beautiful rainbows I have ever seen. I just wanted to stand there and stare at it.

When I walked into school everybody who saw it was commenting about its beauty. It was causing everybody to smile and feel good. My attitude was completely transformed. I was excited and asking everybody, "Did you see it?" So what was it about a rainbow that changed my attitude and the attitude of those around me so quickly?

The answer is simpler than you might realize. The rainbow is the sign or the seal of a covenant between God and mankind. A covenant, you know, is a promise. This promise is from God, who is certainly a very reliable source and one we can trust. We do not use seals in America because we do not have kings, so let me explain a seal's purpose. If a king puts his seal on something it is a form of a guarantee that he will do what is written on the agreement. So the rainbow is our seal that God will keep His promise that He made to Noah.

The promise, as you will remember, was that God will not destroy all life through a flood. It is encouraging to know that God really does care about the world. Often people portray God as this tough, mean spirit who is looking for every opportunity to shoot lightning bolts at us. I think that the promise of the rainbow reveals the truer nature of God's heart towards the world. God cares about us and He is concerned about our lives.

Seeing a rainbow should remind us of two things about God. First, God will judge the world. We don't need to worry about that because He is the most fair and impartial judge. Second, God is a God of mercy and grace. God has provided a way for us to receive his mercy and grace, through Jesus His son. If we repent from our sins, God will forgive us, and He will pour out his mercy and grace on our lives. It's there, free for the asking.

God knows that we will all feel gloomy sometimes. Seeing the rainbow sure made me feel great. I knew that God was with me and concerned about me. The rainbow is God's way of saying, "I care." The Bible is full of promises from God. Some are conditional, meaning that we have to fulfill our end of the bargain. Many of the promises are given unconditionally for us. For example, God's love is unconditional and free for everybody. My encouragement to you is to read the Bible and learn more about the promises God made to you.

Storms

I was driving home alone the other night when off in the distance I noticed a storm. My first thought was that I could easily beat that storm home. As I continued to drive home I watched the flashes in the otherwise tranquil evening sky. I could not hear any rumbles of thunder nor was there any wind from the approaching storm. Even though I was driving towards the storm and it was moving towards me I was not afraid because it was over there.

As I pressed on towards home the sky began to brighten more with bigger flashes of lightening. The trees and bushes began to sway as the wind from the storm began to blow. The faint sound of thunder began to grow in my ear. I was still fifteen minutes from home when I came to the conclusion that I would have to drive through the storm. I was beginning to feel afraid and I wanted to turn my car around and drive away from the storm. I am not sure what I was afraid of but I believe it was the fear of the unknown. What did the storm hold for me; wind, bright flashes of lightening, booming thunder, heavy rain and possibly some hail?

With a prayer on my lips, I pushed onward hoping to get home quickly. As I drove through that storm all my fears became reality, all except the hail. I breathed a sigh of relief as I pulled into my driveway. I gathered my things and made a mad dash for the house. Once inside the storm did not seem quite as terrible as it did in my car. I was finally in the safety of my home.

We can expect very similar experiences in our spiritual life. It seems we don't become overly concerned as long as the storm is in someone else's life. But let that storm come a little closer to our lives and we will fight or run away. Why? Life has "sunny days" and "stormy days." Why do some storms scare us so badly? I think it's a combination of the fear of the unknown and having the faith that God will sustain us in our weakness and inadequacy. God has helped many generations whether the same type of storms you and I experience in our lives. That alone should bring us some comfort. God knows how to guide and comfort us in the tough storms of life.

As far as the fear of the unknown, we need to learn to trust

God. He knows what is in the storm for us and He promises that He will not bring more than we are capable of bearing or handling. God is testing our faith to see how we will respond to the storms in life. When we see the storm on the horizon will we run from God thinking He is unable to help us through it? What we need to do is run to God and allow Him to provide the comfort protection that we need. We need to allow God to walk with us through the storm. If we consistently run to God, He will teach us about Himself and His unfailing love for us. Then, because of our experiences, we will understand His faithfulness. Once we understand God's faithfulness in the storms of life, we will have a testimony of His great love to share with others.

It is so comforting for me to be in my house when a storm is raging outside. While I am there the storm just doesn't seem as bad. Similarly, when I go through the storms of life I have a place to run for comfort and protection. In my Father's strong and protective arms the storms of life just don't seem as bad.

I have found in my life that when a storm starts
to rage around me, God will do one of two things.
Sometimes he will get up and speak to the storm,
"Quiet! Be still!"
like he did in Mark 4:39.
other times I have found that He will allow the storm to rage on.
In those times he comes to me and comforts me
with the peace that surpasses all understanding.

Snow is a Spiritual Thing

I can't believe it finally happened. It snowed! I almost thought that nature forgot how to make the stuff. I wish it had snowed a little more. However, I am glad we did not get three, two or even one foot of it.

If you haven't figured it out, I love snow. I have always loved snow even from childhood. One of the family jokes was that my dad was going to send me to college at the University of Buffalo. Buffalo is famous for huge snowfalls because it is situated on Lake Erie. If surrounding areas get 8-12 inches, Buffalo would get two feet.

When the forecasters say there is a chance for snow I get more excited than anyone could believe. I am constantly looking out the window trying to be the one to spot the first snow flake. The big snow storm that moved up the East coast this past weekend almost forgot to give us any snow. In fact, my wife and I had given up on the snow. I figured if it hadn't changed to snow Friday night it probably wouldn't change to snow during the day on Saturday. So we headed out to the mall Saturday afternoon for lunch. Imagine our surprise when it started snowing before we arrived at the mall. I figured we had plenty of time before the roads would get bad, so we continued on our way to the mall. I noticed it was starting to stick as we walking into the mall. I quickly changed my mind about having "plenty of time" when I heard thunder. A thunder snowstorm can really put down the snow fast similar to a spring thunderstorm.

There is a spiritual significance to snow. The whiteness of snow in the Bible is symbolic of purity, holiness, and innocence. Isaiah prophecies in chapter 1 verse 18, "Though your sins are like scarlet, they shall be as white as SNOW; though they are red as crimson, they shall be like wool."

There is an analogy between the formation of snow and the cleansing of our sin. Snow forms in the upper levels of the atmosphere as particles of water attach themselves to specks of dust and then crystalize into beautiful snowflakes. We are all sinners in God's eyes "...for all have sinned and fall short of the glory of God." (Rom. 3:23) God takes the little insignificant specks of dust (us) and through the shed blood of Jesus makes us pure. For we "...are justified freely by his grace through the redemption that came by Christ Jesus." (Rom. 3:24) Then God clothes us with beautiful robes of righteousness, the snowflake around the speck of dust.

Can you see why I like snow? As I watch the earth receive its mantle of white, I am reflecting on my own robes of righteousness that I will be wearing someday. Have you ever noticed how the snow covers the mess in your yard with a garland of white freshness? That's what God's righteousness does. It covers all the sin and rottenness in our lives with God's purity.

The pristine snow gently drifting to its destiny is like God's undeserved mercy falling on you and me. Many people think that we have to earn God's love, mercy, forgiveness and righteousness. These are free gifts to all who will receive them.

I hope you had the chance to have a snowball fight, make a snowman and an angel in the snow. Maybe you were lucky enough to enjoy some hot chocolate while sitting next to a roaring fire, reading a good book. If you didn't get the chance to do any of these, give it a try next time Old Man Winter pays your yard a visit.

Whatever you happen to be doing the next time it snows, I hope you will take time to reflect on God's grace and mercy. God's grace and mercy are deeper than the ocean and they make you whiter than snow. Thank the Lord Jesus Christ.

Cleanse me with hyssop,
and I will be clean;
wash me, and I will be
whiter than snow.
Psalms 51:7

The Front Page!

I wanted to write a story about the Opossums at the Cosgrove's house. I talked to Kate Dickson, the editor of The Stanly News & Press (SNAP), about getting some pictures and she sent the photographer out. I came home and began the creative process of writing the story. Even though I had only been published in the paper a few times, I knew the style the article was supposed to possess. I wrote the story from a biblical standpoint. When I took my story to the SNAP I thought they would chop it to pieces. I wasn't even sure they would run a story like mine.

A few days later I called the paper to see if the editor had decided to run the story. Kate said it would be out on the following Thursday. I went by the SNAP's office to pick up a copy to see how it came out. I nearly fainted when I saw it on the **FRONT PAGE!**

The following article is my first, and only, front page article. I would like to share these additional comments about the opossums. They were eventually set free. They lived in Richard's barn while they stayed with the Cosgrove's. The survivors were taken to a park to be released. The Cosgrove's spread plenty of food around the area they released them in to give them a good start. Here's hoping they made it!

(PS: Thanks to the opossums and the Cosgrove's for giving me the chance to appear on the **front page!!!!**)

Opossum

It's not very often that you get the chance to meet a real live
Good Samaritan. The Cosgrove family of Richfield is a modern
day example of the Good Samaritan story. One day Richard was
walking down the road when he saw an opossum that had been hit
by a car. He almost walked past it when he noticed some
movement around the dead animal. What he discovered was six
baby opossums trying to nurse. Richard had compassion for them
and decided to bring them home.

His children David, Emily and Frances were ecstatic. Dad
explained to his children that they would only stay with them until
they could survive on their own ...Good Luck!! The children have
adopted them and play with them constantly. The children named
their new playmates; Caroline, Felimateen, Hiroko, Johnny, Travis
and Peter. Travis and Peter died shortly after adoption.

The Cosgrove's have turned this into a real learning
experience. They feed the little guys some milk out of an eye
dropper and a little hamburger two or three times a day. Opossums
eat meat and vegetables and Emily said one of the babies ate some
of her apple. The whole family gets involved, Kay, Richards wife,
feeds the babies and Sam, the family dog, washed them off.

David says he likes to hold them, play with them in the tree
fort, and just pet them. Being nocturnal they sleep most of the day
except when the children are playing with them. According to
Richard, these opossums probably won't be nocturnal because the
children play with them all day.

Frances admits that she and her sister dressed them up in
Barbie clothes once. The cutest thing I saw the kids do was wear
the opossums as earrings. They took the long tails, which are
strong, and wrapped them around their ears and they hung down
like big moving earrings.

One night one of the opossums played the game for which
they are famous. Just before bedtime the children were doing one
last head count and came up one short. They looked all over the
house trying to find the missing one. Then they looked in the

garage with no luck. Finally, they heard something while they were searching around the tree fort. After making several funny sounds the little guy crawled out from under the platform. The baby was very glad to join the rest of the family.

They keep the opossums wrapped up in a blanket and in a cage to protect them. The opossums are the only marsupials native to North America. Marsupials have small babies. They are about the size of a kidney bean. When they are born they crawl up the mother's stomach and get into her pouch. They stay in their mother's pouch until they are about two months old. Then they come out and stay close to the mother for several more weeks before striking out on their own. Other related marsupials are the kangaroo and the panda.

Grandpa Cosgrove, who has also gotten involved with raising the opossums, says they are related to the armadillo. Both of them have tails without fur. He says that both animals have to be careful of the cold weather or their tails could freeze.

After holding the little guys I have to agree with Richard, who says, "They are cute in an ugly sort of way." The whole experience reminded me of my own youth. I use to raise hamsters for the local pet store. I remember having as many as thirty in my room at one time. It was a good experience for me to raise the hamsters, just as I am convinced this will be a good learning experience for the Cosgrove kids too.

I think that the children will learn to help those who are in need around them. In the story of the Good Samaritan it was the Jewish person's worst enemy who helped him. All the people who should have helped walked past him. If only we could get past all those barriers we put up; skin color, nationality, educational level and those who are in need around us, then we could all be Good Samaritans. I believe there are three young children who are going to grow up to be like their parents and become...Good Samaritans.

"Which of these three do you think was a neighbor
to the man who fell into the hands of robbers?"
The expert in the law replied,
"The one who had mercy on him."
(The Good Samaritan)
Jesus told him,
"Go and do likewise."
Luke 10:36 & 37

WEEDS

Everyone who has owned some property has pulled some weeds in their lives. If you have a vegetable garden like I do then you probably pull more weeds than you would like to admit. It seems to me that weeds grow better than the vegetables. They always seem to grow so well in flowerbeds and in vegetable gardens. My wife often reminds me they grow in the yard too. I guess I just don't mind them growing in the yard as much as I do in the garden.

In recent years, I have planted my rows farther apart so I can run my tiller down the path. The problem is I still have to pick weeds that are growing in the vegetable rows. During the long hours spent pulling the weeds out I feel as though God has taught me some valuable principles that I want to pass on to you.

Weeds begin their lives small and almost unnoticed. They sometimes even look like the plants that you want to grow, sort of a disguise to throw you off. Sin gets its start in our life in the same way. It's the small things that go unchecked that have an effect on us. If we don't repent of our little sins they will grow up to be big problems.

Once the weeds have a start they put on a growing spurt that causes them to become taller and stronger than the plants you want to grow. They produce shade which begins to stunt the vegetables growth. They begin to take the food and nutrients away leaving very little for the good plants - the vegetables. A spiritual parallel can be drawn from this. Once sin goes unchecked it takes over. People begin devoting more time and energy to the things they want to do than the things God wants them to do. It's like gossip. Someone is told one thing about a person and when they retell the story they embellish it. They cause it to grow so it shades the truth. If sin is keeping the "Son's" rays from shining in your life then you will not be growing in the Lord.

Meanwhile, there is another battle going on underground at the root level. In order to grow in the Lord people need roots. Roots are the first thing to grow in a plant and that is the source of the plants life and energy. The source of our spiritual strength comes from having a quiet time with our creator every day. Sin in our lives will cause us to stop praying and reading the Bible, which is our spiritual food and fertilizer. Sin will therefore have stolen the source of our strength and weakened us.

Once we stop growing and allowed sin to grow, we find ourselves in the shadow of sin. We are no longer living in the light as Jesus is in the light. Who can save us from the weeds? As Paul writes in Rom. 7:21-8:11, "Thanks be to God - through Jesus Christ our Lord!" Jesus is like a Master Gardener. People must allow Jesus to come in and take the weeds out. This is a very unpleasant process. When we have allowed sins to grow to the place that they are shading us from the good things God intended for our lives they are difficult to remove.

We must trust Him that he will not do anything to hurt us. God knows how to pull the weeds out root and all. Speaking of the root, have you ever pulled on a weed and the top came off and the root stayed in the ground? Then have you noticed how quickly the weed returns? This is when we say to God we are sorry we did something but have no real desire to quit or repent. You are leaving the root in the ground. At the first opportunity the weed or sin will return and you will be living in the darkness again.

Once we have received God's grace and mercy we need to return to the things we know and we should be doing ... praying and reading the Bible. That way we can grow and shade the ground and thereby prevent the weeds from having the opportunity to grow up again.

I encourage you to pray and read your Bible every day. It's the only way you can truly know your Master Gardener and savior, Jesus. Jesus longs to meet with you every day. Seek Him and you will find Him and He will help you keep the weeds down. Then His light can shine in and through you.

Bermuda Grass

My wife and I bought some bushes back in late September. We have both been very busy and haven't had the time to get them in the ground. I had to move some blue berries and raspberries before I could plant the new bushes. After that I had to till the new bed in preparation for the new bushes. It was obviously a big job that required a lot of work.

I thought I would be able to complete this large task on a vacation day early this fall. My wife knew I could never complete the work in one day. She says I always under estimate the time required to get a job done. She is usually right. All I accomplished was transplanting my berry bushes and tilling up the new bed. It was a few weeks later when I finally got the new bushes planted.

The place that I planted the new bushes was full of Bermuda grass. My wife and I believe Bermuda grass is a curse from the fall of man. My father-in-law says that if you spray it with Round Up, dig it up and allow it to dry out then burn it, you still won't kill it. He says wherever the smoke goes the Bermuda grass will come back.

Having to deal with the Bermuda caused me to think about how much it is like sin. You may think that I have strange perspective on things. The truth is, most writers do.

Anyway the Bermuda grass reminded me of sin. Anybody who has pulled Bermuda grass knows that it has long, tough roots. They go down deep and cross long distances. As it spreads out it puts down new roots and grows new blades of grass. I have observed Bermuda grass in my yard move into an area and completely choke out all other forms of grass.

Likewise, sin sneaks into our lives and then it puts down roots. If we are watchful, we will see sin trying to sneak in and before it can take root we will remove it through repentance. If we allow the simplest sin to go unrepentant then that sin will take root in our lives. After the original sin takes root, other sins can start to sneak in and grow too. As each sin goes unrepentant it grows and attracts more sin.

The result is a sin filled life. Then if you decide to clean up your act it is much more difficult. Just like the Bermuda grass when sin is allowed to go unchecked it becomes almost impossible to remove. It is possible to make some quick short term changes, but the sins still have roots and desires that are deeply planted in your life.

So what is the solution? The solution is twofold. One, if your life is full of sin right now, then you need to go to the cross of Christ where you can repent and have the burden of sin removed. When Christ does the forgiving and cleaning in your life, he will take the sin out root and all. This is not to say that you will never be tempted in that area of sin again, you will just need to follow step two.

So what is step two? Step two requires that you watch your life and keep your guard up against sin. When you are being tempted pray and ask Christ to help you. Remember that Jesus can identify with you because He was tempted in every way. Then if you fall, repent quickly before it grows and takes root.

Probably all of us have some Bermuda grass in our lives. We all have to work night and day keeping watch over the yard in our soul. Remember prayer and repentance will keep the Bermuda grass down.

I encourage you to keep watch over your life. Everyone sins and everyone needs to repent. Keep up your daily quiet time. That will be the source of your strength which will help keep the weeds down. Good luck and God bless.

Orion Pointing to the Lord?

I walked outside the other night into a cold crisp winter's evening. I looked up and was glad to see the stars shining brightly. The first constellation I looked for was Orion. He is one of my favorites.

Don't misunderstand my love for the night sky to imply that I am into Astrology. Astrology is a type of idolatry because it puts more importance on the creation rather than the creator. I am not into signs or horoscopes for the same reason. I look up and enjoy the stars and consider the wonder of God's creation.

The reason I like Orion so much is that it reminds me of the importance of my armor. The purpose of the armor is to help us take our stand against all the temptations, troubles, and schemes the enemy can throw at us. Why is Paul urging us to put on the full armor of God? Because the Kingdom of God is in battle with the Kingdom of Satan. Even though we are on God's side and we will eventually win, we need to know how to do battle because we could lose some of the little ones.

There is one other important thing to realize before we put on our armor. We are not fighting each other. The Baptist are not fighting the Catholics or the Pentecostals. We are all brothers and sisters in Christ. We are also not doing battle against non-Christians. Our battle or our struggles are against, "the rulers, against this dark world and against the spiritual forces of evil in the heavenly realms." Our battle is a spiritual one against Satan and his adversaries.

Seeing Orion in the night sky reminds me that I need to put on my spiritual armor. The first thing I notice when I look at Orion is the belt. How appropriate because the belt stands for truth. Jesus said, "I am the way, the truth and the life. No one comes to the Father except through me." (John 14:6) So when we are putting on the belt of truth, we are putting on Jesus. When people look at me or my writing I hope they see the truth of Jesus.

The next easy to identify part of Orion is his shield. Our shield is called, "the shield of faith, which (we) can extinguish the flaming arrows of the evil one." You know it is the evil one's desire to shoot us down and destroy our faith. That's why we need to pick up our faith like a shield to protect us from the enemy. We need to trust and believe in God knowing he will protect us as we go through difficult times in our lives. No other religion or god promises that.

Orion wears a small sword on his belt. I like to think of a large powerful sword when I contemplate the armor that I wear. The sword of the spirit represents the word of God. I believe that the more I read and study His word and apply it to my life the better skilled I become using the sword.

The other parts of the armor are peace on our feet, the breastplate of righteousness and the helmet of salvation. I will probably talk about the importance of these in a later column but I wanted to mention them for a purpose. All of the parts of our armor are used for protection except for the sword of the Spirit. The sword is our only offensive weapon. This makes learning, understanding and obeying the word of God even more important.

The way we stand up against the temptations is by knowing, believing and trusting the word of God. If we will remember when Jesus was tempted in the wilderness he quoted scripture (the sword of the Spirit) to defeat the temptation. The only way we can overcome temptation in our lives is by knowing the word of God. The only way we can know the word is by spending time reading, studying and memorizing the word.

It is amazing how the simplest things remind us of the Lord. I encourage you to look for God in everyday things. If I can be reminded of Him while looking at the stars, then we should be able to find Him in the sunrise, the beauty of flowers or in the love and care of a dear friend. I believe God wants us to find Him in these places as well as discovering Him in his word.

Do everything without complaining or arguing,
so that you may become blameless and pure,
children of God in a crooked and depraved generation,
in which you shine like stars in the universe
as you hold out (or on to) the word of life...
Philippians 2:14 - 16

Super Armor for Christians
from the Super Bowl

I usually try to start working on my column on Sunday night. I usually think about the topic earlier in the week, then on Sunday I begin to formulate the ideas on paper. This past Sunday, like most Americans, I was watching the Super Bowl. I am not an avid sports fan, but I do like to watch the big games.

Sunday evening after the game was over I sat quietly and reflected on several battles on a different front. The first thing I noticed was how peaceful and quiet our house is when the TV is off. The game has a constant road going on, plus the announcers never shut up. This reminded me that we need to put the protective armor of peace on our feet. Paul encourages us to spread peace everywhere we go. There is so much division, dissension and disagreement in the world and in the church. We need to work on spreading peace. Our peace, which surpasses all understand, comes from God who will be with us in every circumstance.

The players looked like they were experiencing anything but peace as they ran the ball up and down the football field. I noticed as I watched the game that many of the guys were taking some hard shots to the head. The helmets they wear must be good ones to protect their heads from injury. We as Christians must put on our helmet of salvation to protect our minds from spiritual injury. The enemy attacks the mind telling us we are not good enough to be God's children, or that we aren't worthy of His love. He even tells us we have committed some unforgivable sin. This is when we need to put on our helmet of salvation and remember that our name is written in the Lamb's Book of Life. We are God's children and He loves us very much. We need to see it like a football game. God is our coach and if we listen to his directions and read his plan book, then we will win the battle in the mind.

The players are well equipped with padding to protect them from injury. The shoulder pads will protect the shoulders and chest areas. We, the soldiers of Christ, have a breastplate of righteousness to protect our chest. If we attempted to stand on our own righteousness, the enemy would easily crush us. The Bible clearly says that no one is righteous on their own. Our righteousness comes from Christ. Jesus, the perfect one, bore our sins on the cross. He paid the price so we can approach the Father because of Christ's righteousness. God does not see us because of our sin, instead he sees Jesus in us.

Why have I written about the armor of God the last couple weeks? (Eph. 6) Christianity is not a wimp's faith. God is looking for people of all ages who will fight the good fight of the faith. Many begin believing in Jesus but few follow through on that belief to a personal relationship with a living God. If God truly loves us, like parents love their children, then He wants us to grow up and become mature Christians. That means that He will put us in tough circumstances to see if we will trust Him. In order to get through the tough things we need to put on the armor so we can fight the battle of faith.

I encourage you to pick up your play book, the Bible, and study it. God has a wonderful plan for your life which includes some tough battles. So pick up the football and turn toward the goal, pick up your armor and fight the good fight, put on your running shoes and run the race to completion, keep the faith. Then you will receive the crown of righteousness and the gift of eternal life.

Servants are Seeds

Have you eaten your first month-watering garden tomato yet? What about those delectable ears of corn? Certainly you have enjoyed some beans and squash. Has anybody had any okra yet? This is the time of year all gardeners dream about, the harvest season.

Summer has almost always been my least favorite time of the year. The one and only thing I liked until recent years was the fact that school was out. Now there is one more thing that makes summer wonderful, you guessed it, the garden. I know that tomatoes require lots of heat and sunshine to do their stuff, so I guess I'll put up with it.

Some of my early crops are beginning to finish up. After the early crops are finished I replant with vegetables that will finish up before the fall frost. I plant things like corn, beans and sunflower seeds. I really enjoy watching things grow in my garden and it keeps me out of trouble.

Several weeks ago I went out and got some new seeds to replant my garden. As I was holding these seeds several of Jesus's teachings about seeds went through my mind. The first and most obvious was the parable of the sower. I have been harvesting things like corn and beans and noticing how much return I get from just one seed sown in good soil.

There is something I have also concluded about planting seeds that I feel is valuable. When I plant corn I put out way more seeds than can grow in my rows. After the plants are up I thin them. In the kingdom of God, we should over seed spiritually, like I do with my corn, in order to get a good harvest. I think some people work hard to prepare the soil for spiritual planting but then they only put out one or two seeds. When the harvest comes they wonder why others have such a large yield and they are bringing in so little. You harvest spiritually in proportion to what you plant.

Jesus also said that for seed to produce any harvest it must fall to the ground and die (John 12:23-26). Jesus taught throughout His ministry that we must die to ourselves and live for Him.

Imagine with me that people are seeds. I have to admit that is a funny thought, but consider it. If we live only to please ourselves, we are missing our call. I can imagine a seed living in luxury, having a nice cottony bed to rest on. The seed would never allow itself to get dirty because that would change its life and the seed does not want change. It would want to protect itself from water too because that might cause it to change. A seed like this one is living a selfish life. What will happen to this seed? It will dry out, crack and become useless. Eventually it will die and it will not fulfill its purpose.

However, the seed that serves the Lord would want to lay its life down. It wants to get into the dirt and welcomes the water. These are the agents of change and the servants of God know that God will only bring those changes necessary to fulfill His purposes in their lives.

The servant of God knows that as he lays his life down in the dirt allowing himself to be buried and watered that something strange and wonderful will begin to take place. As the servant begins to pray and read God's word, roots will start to grow out of his feet. If he continues in these good habits soon he will feel something burst from inside and begin to push upward. Suddenly he will feel the sun's warm rays shining on the first leaves of his life. Then through obedience and submission to Jesus as Lord the servant will grow larger and begin to produce fruit.

Consider how the two seeds finished their lives. The selfish one ended up shriveled up and it was useless. The second seed doesn't look at all like it did in the beginning. In fact, it has grown into a plant with fruit. Inside the fruit are the seeds, seeds that look identical to the original seed that began the whole process by laying its life down. The second seed fulfilled the purposes of God by producing fruit in its life.

If you are looking at your spiritual life and find that little or no fruit is being produced, then let me urge you to lay down your life completely. A servant of God should be able to see some fruit from his labor. God will not allow you to see all the fruit you produce, lest you become proud. God desires that we be fruitful and when we are it makes him proud.

Don't you want God to be proud of you? Don't you want to hear, "Well done my good and faithful servant. Enter your Father's rest," when you arrive at heaven's doors? Then I encourage you to lay your life down completely and fulfill the purposes of God in your generation.

Missionary Seeds

Last week I wrote about seeds in a garden being similar to Christians living out their lives. This week I would like to take it a step farther and talk about our missionary purpose within our local church and abroad.

It is part of my belief that all seeds (Christians) start off in pots. Then the Lord will decide where he needs us to go. The location may be familiar (your church from childhood) or it could be anywhere in the world. We (the plant) must remember wherever we go the master gardener has placed us there. He will have chosen the spot knowing that we (the plant) will bear fruit and fulfill His purposes.

Once God has transplanted you, you have to start growing and begin the process of producing fruit. Your garden could be a lush beautiful place, a dry difficult place or it could be like my vegetable garden, full of weeds. Wherever He sends us, we must remember the enemy will be trying to prevent us from being effective and bearing fruit.

What are the purposes of the believer in the body, wherever he or she is planted? The paramount purpose of all believers is know and love the Lord our God. Nothing takes precedence over that. The next most important purpose for believers in the body is prayer. Without prayer nothing of any value will occur within the body of Christ. Prayer is the foundation for any and all the works of God, period!

Everybody knows that we need pastors and elders to lead the church. They are our guides or shepherds. The key to remember about them is that they are plain ordinary people who stumble like the rest of us. We need to keep them off pedestals and in our prayers. The enemy desires to smite the shepherd so he can scatter the sheep. Scattered sheep are easier to pick off than those with shepherds.

Paul expresses the need for prophets in the Bible. It seems sad to me that many churches today don't believe in the gift. Why can't someone find out the heart or mind of God and impart that to the body? A prophet may know of something in the future or they may know the will of God in a particular situation. There are numerous examples of prophets in both the Old and New testaments. Why not in today's church?

Paul writes that there should be apostles within each church. The term Apostles has many definitions including the twelve Disciples of Christ. Several sources I checked define apostles as one sent with a special message on a mission. This could imply our present day missionaries. Every church needs to be reaching out to those who are lost. It's second only to prayer in importance.

There are some people who are gifted in evangelism, like Billy Graham. Everybody can fulfill the call of evangelism if we are willing to step out of our comfort zones. The world is starving for the words of life the gospel offers. Yet so many of us fail to take the bread of life and the cup of new wine and give it to those who need it.

There is a vast need for teachers and friends for our youth today. Within the church the adults often neglect the youth, because they are busy fellowshipping with one another. Young people today need godly examples. There are plenty of worldly ones if no one in the church is willing to do it. Shouldn't we be concerned about raising the next generation?

Now, I know your initial reaction. "I can't do that! Look how imperfect I am." God is looking for willing people. God already knows that you are less than perfect. Pastors, preachers and ministers feel that way every day. Besides young people tend to only see the good in you and they want to emulate it. We have the responsibility to teach them the ways of God. "Train a child in the way he should go and when he is old he will not depart from it." Does that sound familiar? It should!

There are plenty of roles and abilities that I have not touched upon. There are secretaries, custodians, gardeners, ground keepers, treasures, administrators and on and on. There are many different roles and responsibilities within a church that are opportunities for us to serve. I have never been to a church yet that announces, "Please do not help with this. We have too many volunteers."

Every person in the body of Christ can and must play an important role. There is no one role that is more important than any other. Find your niche within the body and be a blessing to those

God puts in your path. Suddenly you'll discover God using you in ways you never expected. God bless you as you fulfill His purpose in your generation.

Go into all the world and preach the good news to all creation.
Whoever believes and is baptized will be saved,
but whoever does not believe will be condemned.
And these signs will accompany those who believe:
In my name they will drive out demons,
they will speak in new tongues;
...they will place their hands on sick people,
and they will get well."
Mark 16:15 - 18

Divorce

Many of my regular readers are not aware that I come from a broken home. My parents separated when I was nineteen and divorced when I was twenty four. My parents had a nice nest egg set aside for their old age, now the lawyers have most of it. Their divorce was painful for all involved.

Now that I am on this side of divorce I can understand more clearly God's statement in Malachi 2:16 "I hate divorce" says the Lord God of Israel. Divorce tears a man's and a woman's love apart. The resulting shock waves tear the foundations of families to pieces. The pain that occurs because of break-ups lasts for many years.

What I hope to accomplish from writing on the subject is to build a better understanding of the perceptions and feelings of children as they go through the process. I plan to approach the subject from several different angles as noted by the subheadings. Please understand that these are my own personal observations and experiences, your experiences may be different because your circumstances may be different.

I hope that by opening up my life you may find peace of mind knowing that your feelings are "normal" for your situation. I hope that this will bring insight and healing to you. I also hope this will help give you the strength to endure. Believe me there were many times that I did not think I was going to make it. The pain can be paralyzing at times.

One final thought before I begin. My parents were very much in love when I was a child. I knew they loved each other by their actions. I also feel very fortunate that I HAD a great childhood. I have so many wonderful memories of my childhood I know I would be willing to live it all over again (All except the separation and divorce part). Much credit goes to my parents for providing a good loving home to grow up in. For that I am truly grateful to God and to them.

The Announcement to the Family

My Dad chose to, or was assigned to, tell me of the impending doom. I am the third child but my Dad chose to tell me first in the family. I am not sure why he chose to tell me first. I think he hoped to take advantage of my positive outlook on life to be a stabilizer for the other children. In any case, I was the first to learn about the upcoming events.

My dad asked me to go have a beer with him. I did drink some at the time so I accepted. I knew something was up because we had never done anything of the sort before. I was heading off to college in a few weeks so I knew he wanted to talk about something serious. I thought maybe he was going to give me some fatherly advice or tell me about the "birds and the bees." (My Dad, like most parents, is very uncomfortable with that subject)

I don't remember much about the conversation that night. I think I wanted to forget it, you know, hope it would never happen. I do remember my dad telling me that he was going to be moving out. He explained that mom and he had drifted apart. I asked the reasons why. He picked up a salt shaker and said the reasons were as many as the grains of salt in the salt shaker. (Now, whenever I pick up a salt shaker his comments from that night flood my mind. Needless to say I don't use much salt.) He was, in his own way, trying to explain to me that there was not just one reason or cause for their separation.

My father told me one fib that night that bothered me. Many parents used this fib to try to soften the blow and keep hope alive. He said that this separation was to be for about six months so they could try to work on their relationship. He held out a false hope that I clung to as a life preserver. It was the one positive thing in the midst of a sea of negatives. Maybe, just maybe things would work out.

The truth was, at least in my mind, he had no intention to ever try and work it out. I think if he had wanted to work it out he would have stayed right there and worked on it. It is that "fib" that many parents tell their children that ultimately hurts the most.

Parents are trying to ease the pain, which is a noble and loving thing to do. The problem is the children hold onto that as gospel and expect their parents to WORK at it.

The fact of the matter is that "fib" makes the blow of the separation or divorce last longer. The child will hold onto the idea, "maybe my parents will get back together" instead of trying to heal from the brokenness. The pain of always holding on to the potential reconciliation keeps the divorce wounds open and bleeding. It is far better to tell the children, "No, I do not think we will get back together. Even though I know miracles can always happen, I seriously doubt it will in this case." That still leaves a small door of hope but seems much more final. The finality of the marriage, and the realization that it probably won't change, will be the birthing place of the healing process.

I personally held onto that "fantasy" for several years. This was bad, again because the healing could not begin until I put that dream to rest. Once I did decide they would never get back together, I had to go through another period of pain and brokenness. So go ahead and give it to them straight and if a miracle does happen it will be sweeter and better.

The First Time Dad Was Not Home

I attended the local community college after high school. After one year I transferred to James Madison University. My father told me that he would leave sometime after I left for JMU. Basically, he said that he would not be there when I came home. Ouch!

I snuck home a couple times before he left but by Thanksgiving he moved out. For both the Thanksgiving and the Christmas holidays my mother invited my father over to our house. I know her goal was to ease the pain of the separation for the holiday season. It worked. Thanks Mom and Dad for doing this for us.

When I came home for the summer, it was time to accept that Dad was just not around. Tough reality. When I was away at school it did not seem as hard because I wasn't there every day feeling the loss. When I was home for the summer the pain was real and there was no escaping it. My Dad was not coming home to that house any more. I know I cried a lot that summer, but that is very normal too.

How Did I Deal With It?

The truth be known that was probably the most difficult summer of my life. I know I never want to go through anything like that again. When a person is going through pain like that they need an outlet. I had, while away at school, given up drinking. I decided it was not a good Christian witness. Besides, the only two reasons I saw people drink was to get drunk or to get company for the evening, if you catch my drift.

Since I wasn't going to "drown" my sorrows, I needed to discover a way to deal with them. I found the answer in my loving

Heavenly Father's arms. I developed the best habit of my life that summer, I prayed every day. I poured out my heart to my Heavenly Father and I felt like He really listened to me and that He cared. I found that when I spent time with Him I always felt better, so I spent a lot of time with Him.

One of the difficult things I dealt with that summer is the feeling of not having a parent. I have good parents, but they were so emotionally messed up themselves so they couldn't help me. So I turned to my Heavenly Father and asked for help. One day while reading some scripture He showed me this in Psalms 27:10,

Though my father and mother forsake me,

the Lord will receive me.

That verse was a lifeline when I really needed it.

During that summer I learned that "the Lord is our refuge." "He is our strong tower" and "the Lord will accept all who run to Him." I found that the Lord was the answer to dealing with all the emotions of my loss. If you find yourself in that kind of pain I am convinced that He can touch and heal you. I should also point out the healing for this type of pain takes a great deal of time, usually a number of years.

Who's to Blame

One of the things that I thought during the first few months was that it was my fault. I must have done something wrong to cause my parents to separate. Then, if I could change things, maybe they would get back together again. The sad fact is that most children, whatever their age, think this way.

Children of separated or divorced parents listen up; IT'S NOT YOUR FAULT!!!! The fault lies directly and squarely on the parents shoulders. If you are a rowdy child that stays in trouble, your parents would be forced to lean on each other to get through your wild behavior. So your behavior has nothing to do with your parents' divorce. If you are a quiet and obedient child, your quietness didn't make your parents quit on their marriage either.

The reasons your parents divorced are unique to their situation. Again, their marriage problems have nothing to do with you as a child. They have not worked at the marriage, or they have not communicated, or they have not been faithful. They created their own marriage problems. You, as their child, are a product of their love. You are not the source of their problem.

Don't put me in the middle!

Divorced or separated parents are awfully curious about their former spouses. If they had taken that much interest in each other earlier they might have stayed together. The problem is the only people they can ask about their former spouse seems to be the children. The conversation goes something like this: (Note: These are NOT exact conversations that occurred. They are just examples of the kinds of conversations that can occur.)

(a conversation with my Dad)
"How's your Mom?"
"She's ok."
"What is she up to?"
"Not very much. You know the usual stuff."
"Is she seeing anybody?"
"No, not right now."

(A conversation with Mom a day or two later)

"Where the heck (*sometimes a different "H" word*) do you get off telling your Father that I'm doing 'nothing'?"

"What?"

"I just got off the phone with your father and he says that you told him that I was doing nothing but sitting on my duff. I'll tell you what; I have been working hard around this house to keep it up. Who do you think washes your clothes and cooks your supper?"

"I didn't tell Dad you were 'doing nothing.'"

"Yeah. Yeah. And don't be telling your Father that I haven't gone out on dates. How do you know that I haven't been out on a date? I could have gone last night while you were working or the other night when you were out with your friends."

"Well excuuuuuuusssssseee me! I'm sorry!"

"Well you better be. From now on don't tell your Father anything about me. Do you understand me?"

"Yes Mom."

*** About five minutes later after tempers have cooled. ***

"What's your father up to?"

"The same. He works all the time."

"Has he met anybody yet?"

"He said he went out the other night."

"Have you met her? Is she nice?"

"I don't know. I haven't met her."

(Sometime later with Dad)

"Where the heck (*again you might substitute the other "H" word here*) do you get off telling your mother I was out with a red head!"

"I didn't tell her that."

"She said you told her I was 'Tom catching' around all the time. I don't live like that and I would appreciate it if you wouldn't tell her stuff like that."

"Dad I didn't say anything like that. I told her you went out but I didn't know who she was or what she looked like."

"Well don't tell your mother anything. I don't want her to know anything about me or my life. Is that clear?"

"Yes dad."
** *About five minutes later once tempers have cooled.* **
"How's your Mom? What is she........."

Do you get the picture? Neither parent wants you to tell the other anything about their lives. All this does is encourage your children to lie. You see, you have to answer your parents when they ask you something or they yell at you for not answering. So you either answer honestly and get yelled at later or your lie now. Guess what children learn to do?

"What's your mom up to?"

"She's really busy. (LIE) She's hardly ever at home." (LIE)

"What's she doing? Has she had a date?"

"She's got something to do all the time. About that date, I don't think she's been out." (LIE)

Or......

"How's your Dad?"

"He's OK." (LIE he just had a bad cold)

"Has he met anybody nice?"

"Not that I know of." (LIE)

"Has he introduced you to any of his dates?"

"No, that's none of my business." (LIE he and his date stopped in where I worked so I could meet her.)

Do you see what I mean about children learning to lie? It is better to leave some subjects alone and keep your kids honest than to put them in places where they have to lie.

My brother came up with a great idea a few years ago that I like a lot. When one parent asks about the other he reminds them of the invention that Alexander Graham Bell discovered, the telephone. "If you want to know something about (mom or Dad whichever is appropriate) there's the phone." I tried that on my parents, and guess what happened? It worked.

The bottom line on this is for the parents. If you want to know about your former spouse call and ask them. Please stop asking your children. It's tough being in the middle.

The Lie

*The following situation actually did
occur to me and I have decided to share
it so others could learn from my mistake.*

It all began with going to get the mail one day. When I
came in Mom asked me if a check was there. I told her no. She
said that if I saw some tax checks to let her know but not to tell
Dad. I asked why she was planning to keep it from Dad. She said
she was going to try to get some money out of the check to help
with the bills.

I am really not sure if I ever saw those checks arrive or not,
but I knew what was supposed to happen if they did arrive. I was
working for my father that summer so he asked me about the
checks from time to time. I told him that I didn't know if they had
come or not. He seemed to get agitated after a while but I felt that
was his problem.

One day he came to the house to pick up my little sister to go
someplace. I am sure he asked my mother where the checks were. I
do not know what took place during that conversation but I know
what followed.

My Dad yelled for me to come down stairs. I came very
quickly because there was anger in his voice. He demanded that I
tell him if I knew anything about the checks. I told him I hadn't
seen them. He asked me if I knew my Mother was planning to hold
them. Well, I knew that, so I stammered over the answer.

At the point my father started to yell at me in full volume. He
asked me what type of Christian I was that told his own father lies.
He was yelling real loud. I tried to go outside to get away from
him. I was afraid. He followed and kept right on yelling at me. He
was yelling so loud that several neighbors came outside to see
what was going on. He made a big scene and it was downright
scary.

My little sister watched him and listened to all the yelling and got scared too. She decided she wasn't going to go with him. That made him even more mad. Both parents yelled at each other very loudly while the neighbors watched and wondered if they needed to call the police. Finally, he stormed out of there.

After I was able to pull myself together, I got up and got out of there. I didn't know where to go. I drove around for a while and ended up at my pastor's house. He was out, but his wife was there and she talked with me. She told me the truth I needed to hear. "You should never have lied. It is wrong to lie to either of your parents, no matter what the reason." It was a hard truth, but I knew she was right.

The lesson from the situation is twofold. One, if you feel your parents are putting you in the middle, tell them. Most parents if they realize that they are putting you in the middle will attempt to stop. Why? They don't want to hurt you any more than you are already hurt. The second lesson is never lie. What I should have done in the situation was told my Dad to call my Mom about those checks. Or when he asked, I could have called my mother on the phone and put my Dad on the line with her. Again, get yourself out of the middle when you can and avoid lying for any reason.

Let's talk about it

If anybody has watched the talk shows they have seen divorced adults and children of divorced parents on them. They pour out their guts that are filled with horrible feelings and thoughts. That is obviously what the hosts want because that draws viewers.

Talking about my parents' divorce was not easy when it first happened. The first person I could bring myself to tell was my girlfriend (who is now my wife). I felt like I was telling her I had leprosy. I thought it was disgraceful and that the world was going to end very soon. My emotions were on the edge, but I didn't want her to see that. She was sensitive and understanding which helped a whole bunch.

Was I bitter and angry with my parents? You bet I was. I was a Christian, but I was not having Christian feelings about my parents at the time. I would never have wanted to appear on one of those talk shows, because I would have said things that are no longer true. I would have said hateful and bitter things that God has been able to heal since then. Once you have said those hateful and bitter things, the memory is never erased for the listener. We have to learn to give those feelings over to God, so he can heal them.

This brings up an important point; concerning parents and children talking about the divorce. I have one parent from each extreme. One parent has hardly ever talked about the divorce. This parent never asked how I was doing in relationship to my feelings about the divorce. I sometimes wondered if this parent cared. Now I realize they were in so much pain they couldn't deal with mine.

My other parent took the opposite extreme. Every phone call and every visit in seemed we had to talk about the divorce. That meant digging up and reliving all that pain all over again. Scars you thought were healing or almost healed were ripped open with every visit. My parents are separated for over twelve years now and this parent still wants to talk about it. That is taxing.

I do not believe either method is correct. I think there should be some conversation in the early stages to try and prevent hostilities and bitterness. As time passes talk about the situation should also pass. While talking about your feelings is very important to healing, continually talking about it can actually prevent healing.

The true healer in divorce is time. It just takes time to get over the pain and sometimes it's tough waiting on it. Parents really desire for their children to move on in life and to get over the pain. They often fail to realize that time is the healer. They want their children to heal quickly, which again is a noble and loving desire.

Discipline

Because parents have a desire for children to heal quickly they tend to lighten up on discipline. Sometimes discipline disappears completely. This is the worst possible thing a parent can do for the child. I have seen it time and time again in the public schools. I'll call a parent over some discipline problem and the parent's immediately excuses their child's behavior because of the divorce. I then ask the parent how long it has been since the divorce. They answer many years ago. My thought: "Your child is pulling the wool over your eyes. They need discipline," but of course, I can't say that.

All children, from stable to divorced homes, need limits and discipline. Often divorced parents will not set limits or discipline their children because they don't want their children to dislike them. Wrong choice again. Every child dislikes discipline, not the disciplinarian. I've had students yell, "I hate you and your class!" Then they turn around and sign up for my class the next year. Children yearn for limits because they are safety nets for their lives.

When I was a small child my parents had a pretty good marriage. When I stepped out of line my mother would spank me or put me in a chair for a while to correct me. I know that many times I yelled at my mother, "I hate you," she often quipped back, "Good. Then I am doing my job." And usually the behavior that she was attempting to correct was corrected. I know I hurt my mother when I yelled, "I hate you!" Sometimes I would say it just for that purpose. Now, looking back on things, I understand discipline is necessary to get the job done.

Question: Did I really HATE my mother? Are you kidding me? I loved and still love my mother very, very much. What I did not like was the spanking or having to sit quietly. *Problem*: If my mother had been divorced when I yelled, "I hate you." That would have hurt even more deeply. She then may have chosen not to discipline me in the future because she wanted me to like her. Big mistake! All children need correction and they will fight it like crazy if they are normal. *Solution*: Set limits and discipline your children. They may say things like, "I hate you!" but those are normal and they will appreciate the discipline in the long run. Also, they will grow up to be well-rounded, well-adjusted and self-disciplined individuals that you will be proud to call your own.

Dealing with the Pain

As I have already indicated, I was bitter and angry with my parents about the divorce. I think that it is pretty common among children of divorced parents. There are two ways to deal with these emotions. I could choose to let the bitterness grow and fester inside me. Then later in life it would come out in some unpleasant and undesirable way. My other choice was to take it before the Lord for healing.

It's like I tell anybody who is hurting over something as big as divorce or death you have two choices: A) You can run to God or B) You can run away from God. That first summer home from college was the toughest. But that is when I turned it all over to the Lord. Now God is mighty and I believe he is capable of instant healing, but He did not choose to instantly heal me. God chose to use time.

I was in a real fix when I arrived home from my first summer vacation without a father. I had just broken up with my girlfriend. I had no summer job and I desperately needed the money for school in the fall. And to top it all off, I had to deal with the emotion surrounding my parents' divorce. Do you think I had a fun summer? It was the toughest summer of my life!

During this summer I gave up my old high school buddies too. They had become drinking buddies and I gave up drinking. Some of them were even using drugs. I did make some new friends from church. We were a real bunch. We were all strong as we encouraged each other in our Christian walk. Since that summer I have talked to the others in that group and we all confess to having the worst, yet the best, summer of our lives. Does that make sense?

Yes it does, when you consider that all of us were spending a whole bunch of time with the Lord and with each other. Pressing in to find a loving heavenly Father makes a great deal of difference on the perspective of problems. God truly cares about our individual human condition. Remember he came to save us one by one. He knows our names and He knows how many hairs we have on our head. We need to know that God desires that we come and pour our hearts out at his feet. So when we encounter deep and painful situations.... we need to run to the Father. In His arms we'll find comfort and peace.

Forgiveness

There is no real delicate way to put this so I'll say it straight out. You need to forgive your parents for the separation or divorce. They are human and they failed. Guess what? You are human and you will fail too (Hopefully not in marriage). You have got to come to a place where you can forgive your parents for their mistake.

Now I know it won't happen immediately. As I have already stated, it will take time to be healed from such devastating pain. But you have a responsibility before God to forgive them. Jesus said, "If you forgive men (your parents) when they sin against you, your Heavenly Father will forgive you. If you do not forgive men (your parents) their sins, your Father will not forgive you." That is very difficult, but they are the words of Jesus.

Again, let me caution you, it will take time. It could take several years to finally come to complete forgiveness, but you must work to get there. In the beginning, it is a daily process of confessing out loud even though you don't feel it in your heart. But let me encourage you, it will come to pass. Hang in there.

Romans 8:28

And we know that in all things (even divorce)
God works for the good of those who love him,
who have been called according to his purpose.

How in the name of heaven can God possible work out anything good from my parents' divorce? He can! Let me share three examples of how He did it.

The first story comes from the Boy Scouts. When I went to college I dropped out of leadership with the Scouts. However, when I came home for my first summer vacation I felt the need to be involved again. When summer camp time came I was working so I couldn't go.

One evening, a few days before the boys were to leave, I got a phone call from the Scout Master. He told me that they really needed some help and he wanted me to come to camp for at least part of the week. I told him no, but that I would think about it. The next couple days as I prayed I began to feel a burden to be at camp. So I called the Scout Master back and told him I could come for the last few days. That was perfect because someone else could only stay there for the first part of the week.

One evening while walking up to supper at camp, I noticed that one of the boys seemed out of it. I asked him what was wrong, and he said I would never understand. I asked him to test me and see if I could understand. Then with tears rolling down his cheeks he told me that when he got home from camp one of his parents was going to be moved out, his parents were separating. My heart broke with his. I knew the pain he felt all too intimately.

I listened to his story and then to his amazement I shared my own. He couldn't believe that someone else had felt that kind of pain. We talked for quite a while sitting on the trail. The one thing I was able to help him understand was that his parents' separation was not his fault. He was convinced that he had done something terribly wrong. It took me a while, but I was eventually able to convince him that it was not his fault.

We ate a late dinner together and continued to share. By the next morning he was back to his usual self and interacting with the other boys. He ended up having a good week. You see God can use bad things to help others. If my parents hadn't separated, I would not have known what to say to the young boy. It is also interesting to note the lengths God will go to in order to get the one in need together with someone who has been there and knows how things feel.

The second story comes from school. There are many stories I can share about the ways that God has used me to encourage teenagers whose parents have divorced. Every year there are several students that I get the opportunity to encourage concerning divorce. However, one story seems to stand out in my mind that I want to share.

Several years ago the guidance counselor decided to get a

group of students together and let them talk about divorce. The group met every other week. The group started at the request of a student and I asked to be a part of it. There was a good degree of openness and confidentiality among the group. I openly shared my experiences with the students and felt like I made some connection with a few of them.

At a recent graduation, I congratulated one of the graduates. He thanked me then said, "Mr. Creamer I will never forget the help you gave me during those group meetings. They made a big difference for me and I really appreciated it." I smiled at him but I was speechless. I did manage to thank him before someone else came over and hugged him.

The final story of how God can use terrible things to help others is the one you have just read. I could never have written this unless I had experienced it. Divorce is terrible, but God is greater than divorce. If we will turn our pain over to God, He can heal our pain. Once healed, He can use us to touch others who are experiencing the same kind of pain.

In Conclusion

Children

What do I want you to remember? If you are the child of parents who have divorced or separated, no matter what age, keep these things in mind. 1) It is not your fault! The responsibility for your parents failed marriage lies directly on their shoulders. Nothing you could have done would have, or could have, changed that. 2) It will take some time to get over the pain of their divorce. Even though Jesus is capable of instant healing, He rarely does in the case of divorce. He allows time to heal you. 3) Keep yourself out of the middle. If your parents start asking questions about their former spouse, tell them to call their former spouse. Parents will ask until you tell them to stop. 4) Never lie to either of your parents even if they tell you to cover for them. Lying leads to worse problems down the road. And finally, Jesus is the only one who can heal the pain. I know I said He often uses time but He is the one who heals over time. Run to Jesus with your pain, He can take it from you.

Parents

If you are a parent who has divorced your spouse try to keep the following things in mind. 1) Stop putting your children in the middle. Stop asking them about your former spouse. If you want to know something, just ask your former spouse. 2) When you tell your children about your failure in marriage, don't leave a door open for reconciliation. Children need the cold hard facts so they can begin to heal from the deep pain. 3) Talk to your children in the beginning about their feelings. Keep a check on them to keep bitterness from forming in their hearts. But give them the space to heal too. 4) Don't put your former spouse down in front of the children. That former spouse is still a parent to the child. You do not want them putting you down. I know you are struggling with bitter feelings but don't share them with your kids. 5) Don't forget children need discipline. Don't let them use the divorce as a crutch. All children hate discipline but they usually love the disciplinarian. Discipline sets limits and guidelines and children need them. 6) Remember that you are suffering from pain too. Don't expect yourself to heal overnight. You have to give your pain over to the Lord too.

The total bottom line, if you are a parent or a child in the divorce process, is that God is in control. If God is in control, then He can work all things together to good, even divorce. Keep your eyes on Jesus and He will lead you through the paths that will bring healing. Don't get discouraged it is a long process to be completely healed.

Love

We are rapidly approaching the holiday that celebrates love, Valentine's Day. Americans will spend millions of dollars over the next few days to show their loved ones that they care. With this in mind, I thought it would be very appropriate to write about love. I know many books have been written on this subject, but I hope to share some of my own thoughts.

The place to begin is with God and Jesus. The Bible teaches that they loved us even while we were lost in our sins. This is where love begins. We must receive from the Father His unwarranted and faithful love. His love is all consuming, healing, transforming and renewing. We must first of all receive this love before we can truly love someone else.

Next we have to understand that love is more than just a feeling. This is probably the reason many marriages end in divorce, because people don't "feel" in love. Love must go beyond a feeling to commitment. You may be very upset or even angry with the one you love but that should not change the fact that you love the person. True love must be put to the test. I believe that God does or at least allows the tests to occur. The Bible says love is patient, which implies that love will be trying at times. That means that we must preserve through tough times. If we do, our love will be stronger and better.

God's love toward us is unconditional. So we need to show unconditional love for those around us, especially those with whom we are the closest.

In order for love to exist there must be a large degree of trust. Trust is based upon confidence, integrity, character and faith. I must have faith in my wife that she won't do anything to hurt our relationship and she must have the same faith in me. Also, each partner has the responsibility to avoid doing things that will raise the other's suspicions. This means that you do not hide things from each other. Husbands and wives should be completely open, transparent and honest. Love will only flourish where trust and Christ are at the center of the relationship.

In order for love to grow each partner must build the other up.

This is important, basic, and very often forgotten. I know that there are times when I need my wife to give me a great big bear hug. Equally, I must give her hugs that let her know that I couldn't make it without her. It's also important that we say "I love you" to each other.

The flip side of the coin is equally important. We should not be spending time putting our spouses down. No one likes to be put down. Can you imagine Jesus insulting you or making you the butt of all his heavenly jokes? That would hurt. Well, it hurts your spouse when you make them the butt of all your jokes. Instead, spend time building your spouse up in front of others. Pay them compliments in front of others and while you are alone. Thank them for doing everyday things. I guarantee it will have a positive effect on your relationship and it will build your love.

Many older men grew up in a time when it was not popular or masculine to let your wife know how you felt. Men, this is the most important thing you can do. You may not feel comfortable doing it, but loving words spoken from the heart mean more than any of us will ever know. You don't need to spread a bunch of mush, just be sincere in expressing your loving feelings. It may be difficult at first, but if you keep practicing it can grow into an excellent habit.

This Valentine's Day take advantage of your chance to express your loving feelings. Instead of just signing your name to the beautiful card you bought, add a few lines of your own. Express your own feelings. Even a simple "I love you and I need you" in your own handwriting can speak volumes to your spouse. Take a few small steps and see if you can't find ways of making every day Valentine's Day in your house.

Easter Baskets of Forgiveness

I grew up in a home where the Easter Bunny made yearly appearances. I was very excited on Easter morning to find my basket of candy. I loved (and still to this day love) Easter candy. When I was a small child I really believed the Easter Bunny came to my house just like Santa Claus.

Certainly I was disappointed to learn that neither Santa nor the Easter Bunny were real. But I do not remember these revelations affecting my faith in God. Even though I was not a Christian as a young child, I did believe in God.

I knew there was a deeper meaning to Easter than baskets of candy. However, I was too young to understand that Jesus died on a cross for me, to forgive my sins. I didn't know I had committed any sins.

Sometimes it is hard to understand and receive the forgiveness of God. It is particularly difficult when you do things you know you should not have done. I often feel like, "OK God, just hit me or something. You know, a good fair punishment for what I did." But then I hear the Father whisper in my ear, "I already did. I put the punishment for your sin on Jesus. He bore your sin on the cross so you could go free."

Talk about your guilt trips. Here I did something against God that I knew I should not have done and he makes his Son pay for it. Then I have double the guilt. So instead of being free from the sin I sit around and feel bad about it. These feelings are not from God.

I want you to understand what is going on. First, the enemy tempts us to commit a sin. We, being weak vessels, commit the sin. Then we walk around with our heads down and become ineffective Christians. You see, the enemy wins. He knows that God has already won our souls, but if he can keep us from being effective witnesses to God's love, then he wins.

Does this mean we should not resist sin because we are going to fail anyway? NO! God tells us that He will not allow us to be tempted beyond what we are capable of standing up against. That means every time we give in to sin, we could have defeated it had we turned away and trusted in God.

We have to trust in God's grace and his mercy. God will give us grace to stand up against the temptations and He will give us His mercy if we fail. God says that if we confess our sins He is faithful to forgive us (giving us His mercy). The amazing thing about God is that He will forgive us for our sin and cleanse us from the guilt.

Our problem is letting Him do it. All that time we walk around feeling guilty is wasted. Jesus already freed us from the guilt; we need to receive God's grace and forgiveness. We all have a hard time forgiving ourselves. That's pride. It's also a lack of understanding of God's grace. Grace is unwarranted favor. There is nothing you can do to earn God's favor, because it's a gift. Grace is also the power to live differently, as an overcomer.

Living for God is a constant battle to do what is right. Jesus knows that sometimes we succeed and win that battle and sometimes we lose. He went to the cross on Good Friday because he knew that sometimes we would fail. Since God requires a sacrifice for our sins, Jesus took our place and became that sacrifice. We don't deserve forgiveness, mercy, or grace but it is ours for the asking.

Total forgiveness is free for anybody and everybody. That is what Easter is all about. Jesus came to give us forgiveness for our sins and a restored relationship with God. Now that our sins are forgiven, He can have fellowship with us. That is the reason God created man, for fellowship.

I hope you have a Happy Easter. Remember that Easter is God's gift of forgiveness and salvation. Take some time this holiday weekend to give God what He wants most from you. Give Him your fellowship and friendship with thanksgiving because you have been forgiven and the guilt of your sin has been washed away.

The Father's Love

I was fortunate enough to be on a men's retreat last weekend. It was sponsored by my church and was held at on a beautiful piece of property located near Asheboro. The retreat had an evening session on Friday and a morning session on Saturday. Over the next few weeks I plan to share some of the insights and thoughts I had while I was on the retreat.

The first thing I want to share was something I saw while I was going for a walk. There is a man-made lake on the property that attracted some Canadian Geese. When I went down to see them there were only two. Originally, there had been six according to the owner. He told me that the male had fought and chased the other four from the lake. When they were gone, the remaining male and female started a nest.

When I walked down to see the geese, I found the male swimming around the middle of the lake. He paid me little attention until two stray dogs came up barking loudly. Then the goose swam closer to the bank and acted as though he was going to attack the dogs. The owner said that the male goose had chased his dogs off on several occasions. After the dogs ran off, the goose swam back to the center of the lake.

As I stood quietly watching, I began to compare the male goose to the Heavenly Father. That goose watched over his companion and those eggs as if his very life depended on it. I think that is the same way the Heavenly Father "broods" over us. I think He allows us to go through life's ups and downs while He keeps His watchful eye on us. In Psalm 34 it says, "The angel of the Lord encamps around those who fear him, and he delivers them." I think the Heavenly Father finds a good vantage point and keeps His eye on us, just like that goose.

There is another scripture in Matthew 10 that reminds me that our Father is keeping His eye on us. It says, "Are not two sparrows sold for a penny? Yet not one of them will falls to the ground apart from the will of the Father. And even the very hairs on your head are all numbered. So don't be afraid; you are worth more than many sparrows." This reaffirms for me that God is watching over us. If He knows the number of hairs that are on our heads, then He knows everything there is to know about us. I don't think He knows this stuff as a trivial fact either, I think this reveals a deep heartfelt concern for us.

While I stood by the lake, I hoped to see the female goose. Initially, I could not see her because she was sitting on the nest. Her nest was on the opposite side of the lake. Once someone pointed out her nest to me I could easily see it. She sat dutifully on the nest keeping the eggs warm and safe.

I think this is an excellent example of a mother's love. Mothers are often not appreciated for the endless hours of sacrifice for their children. Mothers teach their children to walk, run and play. They teach us to eat our food properly. They teach us to wash our hands before we eat. They teach us manners. I can hear my mother saying, "Now what is the magic word?" "Please." "Thank-you." would be my response. Mothers are the ones who will fix that hot soup for us when we don't feel well. Mothers sacrifice a lot and we should let them know we appreciate it.

We should all take a few moments, especially this MOTHERS DAY WEEKEND to tell our mothers how much we appreciate them. I know that I am glad that my mother raised me in a loving environment. She gave me a good set of morals and taught me right from wrong. Now, all that learning wasn't fun, but it has helped me live with more integrity. I think my love and appreciation of nature and especially of God came from my mother. I am glad God gave me a good mother. I hope that she and all of you mother's will have a great Mother's Day!

Thankful for America on the Fourth of July

Happy Birthday, America! It's fun to celebrate America's birthday. Many people celebrate by cooking out and spending time with family and friends. There is usually plenty of food and loads of laughs culminating in a fireworks spectacular. All the flag-waving, people-parading, baseball-flying fun has got to make you proud to be an American.

I know that America has many problems. All anybody has to do is pick up any major city newspaper and it seems full of major American problems. You could also focus on all the world problems because there are plenty of them. It seems that the world and even our very lives are plagued with big problems. But one day a year we set aside our problems and individual differences and focus our attention on the greatest country in the world.

I think we should focus on the blessings that God has poured out on this great nation. We have so many freedoms and rights that many around the world would like to enjoy. I think we often take them for granted; we ought to reflect on them and be thankful.

Take, for example, the freedom of speech. I have the right and the freedom to express my thoughts about God and even publish them. In many places around the world I would be imprisoned and even put to death for writing a column like this one. Yet here in America I can write openly expressing my thoughts, and I appreciate that right.

The freedom of religious expression is also one of those rights that many people in the world would like to possess. Here in America people of various beliefs are allowed to practice their faith without fear. I saw an article in *The Charlotte Observer* the other day that talked about the Muslim religion. I believe they have the right to practice their religion just like I have the right to practice the principles of my faith. I must not inhibit the practice of their religion, and they must respect the practice of mine.

We also have a host of other freedoms and rights such as the right to peaceably assemble, the right to bear arms, the right to peacefully protest the government if we don't like something, the right to privacy and the right to a speedy trial by our peers. We have the privilege of living as free men, women and children in America. Isn't that great!

One of the prized privileges that we possess is the right to vote. We can choose all the elected officials who run our local, state and federal government. There are many people in the world today who do not get these choices. Think of the people around the world who are living in war zones where leaders are fighting for the right to rule. Then there are countries where dictators rule their people harshly. Do you think these people would like the power of choice?

Along with the privileges we have responsibilities that include paying taxes. The biggest responsibility that we as Christians have is to pray for our elected officials. I met one of my state elected officials and he will tell you that he needs our prayers. If he will admit to needing prayers, imagine how much President Clinton needs our prayers.

Regardless whether you like President Clinton or not he needs our prayers to successfully lead our country. I Timothy 2:1-4 tells us that we should pray for those who are in authority over us. In Romans chapter 13 it says that God put the people in authority. This is all the more reason that we need to pray that they will lead our country in godly paths.

There are many more things for which we need to be thankful. I could never include them all in this space. If we want to continue to enjoy this great country we need to pray for those who are in authority and leadership. Please don't forget to include teachers in your prayers, as we are the ones who are trying to prepare our youth to be the future leaders of our great nation.

What happened to Thanksgiving?

Ho, Ho, Ho, Merry Christmas! That is what you will hear if you go to most retail stores. Christmas is in full bloom. The carols are playing and people are busy doing their Christmas shopping. Did we forget something? Think carefully. We just celebrated Halloween and now we are getting ready for Christmas. Have we forgotten a very important holiday?

Yes. Thanksgiving! I think we all get focused on Christmas and forget Thanksgiving. My wife and I were talking about this at dinner last night. After supper my wife caught me looking at the calendar and she asked me what I was doing. I told her I was just noticing that one of my columns would be published on Christmas Eve. She gave me a "gotcha" smile. That's when I realized I was guilty too.

In the Psalms 107 it says, "Give thanks unto the Lord, for he is good; his love endures forever." If you can't think of anything else, thank him for his love and goodness. In Philippians it says "... but in everything, by prayer, and petition, with thanksgiving, present your requests to God." Within our prayers to God we need to remember to thank him for what he has already done. We all need to learn to be obedient to the scripture and be thankful. The way we should begin is to start on Thanksgiving day.

Thanksgiving, in my eyes, should be a time when we stop being so busy and turn to God to express our thanks. There is so much that we need to be thankful for, yet most of us fail to express it. How many times have you sat down to a meal and forgotten to say thanks? I have eaten a number of meals at my brother's house, and on more than one occasion, it was his five year old son that reminded us to return thanks. With Thanksgiving knocking on our door, I thought it would be appropriate to share some ideas on how others thank God on that day.

One family I know says their thanks before they eat. Each member of the family is given a moment to say the things for which they are individually grateful. Personally, I think that would be hard because my mouth would be watering too much. Some families plan a special time of thanks several hours before the big meal. I think that would help me.

There is another family that does something I think is totally unique. They sit down to the big meal and plow right in. There is no prayer at all before the meal. After the meal is over and the dishes have been piled in the kitchen, the family sits down to prayer. There is nothing to distract them (other than that sleepy feeling that comes with a full stomach.) This family is patient with each other because no one is in a hurry to eat. They tell me the prayers are more sincere, meaningful and from the heart.

I personally try to set aside some time that day so I can reflect on the goodness of God and all His blessings. I thank God for all the things he has helped me through in the last year. I also thank Him for all the tough things that I have gone through. It is because of them that I have grown in character and faith. The truth about bad things is that we either grow from them or we run from the lessons they are supposed to teach us.

Whatever you do on Thanksgiving Day, please take some time out of your busy schedule to thank the Father for all the things he has done for you. Thank him for your salvation, your family, a good home, the good food and His faithfulness in your life. Then have a happy turkey day!

Families and the Holidays

The holidays are wonderful, difficult, fun, stressful, happy and tiring. Why do we put so much pressure on ourselves to be together for the holidays every year? With 365 days to choose from, there is an awful lot of pressure put on people to be together for the holidays. Why can't families pick a weekend in the year that does not revolve around a holiday and plan a get together at that time? There would be a whole lot less pressure and everybody could relax.

Since I have become a grown-up, I have come to learn that not all holidays are joyous and happy times. When there are two sets of parents to please, food to be prepared and eaten, packages to buy and wrap, schedules to keep and many miles to be driven. I've discovered it's almost impossible to please everybody. Why can't it change? Why does everybody want to get together on the holiday? Wouldn't it be the same to get together over the holiday weekend? Or the week before or after a holiday? Don't parents of married children realize that children can only be in one place at one time?

This year for Thanksgiving we were expected in two places at the same time. We asked the family for some flexibility, but neither side wanted to give an inch. Of course both sides of the family considered us at fault in the situation because we were trying to please everybody with a compromise. The pressure increased as Thanksgiving neared. We actually considered having four quiet days at home.

Well, through the prayers of a few close friends, God worked a miracle and we were able to make our families happy. AMEN! We also had a nice weekend and enjoyed seeing both our families. But the question still runs through my mind, why do families put so much emphasis on being together for holidays?

One person who listened to my concerns shared her thoughts with me. When people live as far apart as we do in our society it's difficult to get together. When there is a four day weekend families want to take advantage of the opportunity. That makes sense. How often does the entire family get four days off when they can spend time together?

Another friend shared the same kind of feelings about all the rushing around to get from one house to the other. This woman said she and her family did it for four years when both her parents and her husband's parents were alive. She said they often longed for the chance to stay quietly at home. Now she says they wish that their families were around so they could rush around to be with them. I guess we don't appreciate something until it's gone.

One thing I did learn from the weekend is that we are all looking for different things to come out of time spent together. I think everybody wants to share feelings of love and security in the few moments that we share as a family. In a world that changes so rapidly, knowing your family is there for you helps provide security.

I think that families travel long distances to be together so we can laugh, tease each other, catch up on the news and just remember. We want to remember the good things and be reminded that through all the bad things our lives turned out alright. It's also comforting to know that at least our families love and accept us for who we are, not for what we have done.

You know, maybe all that effort that we put forth to get together is worth it after all. We must understand going into the time that it won't be perfect, but we will be together. Ultimately that is what is important about families, being together. Besides, hopefully during the time that you spend together, you will be able to create new memories that will last a lifetime.

Families; sometimes they can be difficult to live with, but I am convinced it would be more difficult to live without them.

Black & White

I had the privilege of shopping at Carolina Place Mall in Pineville a couple of weekends ago. I really enjoyed all the Christmas decorations and the busy people running around doing their Christmas shopping. I particularly enjoyed watching the kids talking to Santa Claus.

While I was watching the kids waiting in line I noticed that there were black and white children waiting to see Santa. I wondered if the children thought about the fact that Santa seems to always be an old white man. Did they ever ask their parents if Santa was white or black? It probably did not matter to those kids as long as he brought lots of presents.

The question about Santa's color got me to thinking more on a spiritual level. Do children of other nationalities and colors ever wonder why Jesus seems to always be portrayed as a white man? Do you realize that Jesus was probably not a white man? He was not a black man either. Jesus was a man with olive tone skin. Jesus was born in the Persian area of the world and it is very likely that he looked like people from that area.

Have you ever met a person from the Middle East? The next time you do notice their skin tone. They are not white or black but a shade in between, an olive tone. Why mention this? What is the importance? Because in the Body of Christ we need to break down the barriers that exist between the races. There seems to be a low tolerance between people of different backgrounds and heritage. The truth is we all have the same heritage, if we are found in Christ.

Jesus came to save all men and women regardless of race. Jesus is color blind. He treats each person, no matter what color, equally. Are we living like Jesus lived and accepting everybody regardless of race? Do you realize when we get up to heaven black people, Asian people and white people are going to be brothers and sisters? Are we treating each other, regardless of race or nationality, as we would our natural brother or sister?

Suppose a local church burned down whose members were from another race. Let's say that when the church received the insurance check it was only enough to pay for the supplies to rebuild the church and the members would have to do the work themselves. Question: Would you be there to help? You might respond, "Well, I can't do any of that type of work." What if they needed baby sitters while the men worked? What if you could make a great big pot of soup for the workers? Do you think you would go lend a hand if you have carpentry skills? Would you pray for them? Would your actions be different if the church members were from the same race?

This is a simple illustration, but it is an example of the truth in many churches. We see a church down the road going through some difficult situation and we often fail to reach out. We look away to our own church and we fail to see their needs. What would Jesus do if he saw a church in need? Would race keep Him from reaching out? Would it keep you from reaching out and offering a hand?

Maybe this would be a good time to reflect on how racism could play a part in how we are judged in the end. Jesus said that people will be divided into two groups. To the group that he sends away from his presence he will say something to this effect: "Depart from me...You saw me in need and you did not help." This group will be shocked and they will respond, "Lord when did we see you in need and we did not come running to help?" Jesus's answer will be, "When you did it not to the least of these, you did it not to me."

During this Christmas season maybe we should stop judging people by their race, their religion and their income. Jesus came to bring light and love to all men unconditionally. Shouldn't we, his servants, do the same thing? Shouldn't we proclaim God's love to all nations and all peoples? What is the greatest commandment? To love the Lord your God with all your heart, mind and soul and to love your neighbor (regardless of race) as yourself.

Christmas the way it ought to be

By the time you read this it will be one week until Christmas Eve. That means you only have one more week to get all that Christmas shopping done. Good luck!

I was talking to my grandmother on Sunday about Christmas when she was child. She says she can remember the house being quiet except for the radio playing wonderful Christmas hymns. She said she remembers having a beautiful Christmas tree and the house all decorated with streamers and paper bells. She also remembered that on Christmas Eve at 11:00 she and her mother would go to mass. She says she misses the simplicity and peacefulness that use to accompany the holidays. She said that she never got very much for Christmas but that didn't seem to matter. She says with all the things out of the way the focus was on the real meaning of Christmas, the birth of the Christ child.

One of the things my wife and I really enjoy doing at Christmas time is going to a Christmas program. We have gone to things like, "A Christmas Carol" and The Young Messiah's Tour. This year we went to the singing Christmas tree in Salisbury. It was a beautiful Christmas program filled with some of my favorite Christmas hymns and carols. For me Christmas music has to be one of my favorite parts of the Christmas season.

One of the good things about a Christmas program is that it allows me to slow down and reflect on the true meaning of Christmas. With all the Christmas cards waiting to be addressed and sent and all the Christmas shopping I have left to do, it's hard for me to slow down at this time of the year. I really need a Christmas program to grab my attention and return my gaze to that little manger where the Holy child was laid.

At the singing Christmas tree program there were people acting out the story as it was being told and sung. The thing that caught my eye was the fact that they used a real baby. They took the baby and wrapped a blanket around his waist and then they laid him in a real manger. The woman playing Mary picked the child up several times and nuzzled him close to her chest. The father stood proudly over the mother and child and glowed with joy at the birth of the baby. Every once in a while, when the baby was in the manger, the father would reach down and tickle the child's feet.

As I watched all this and listened to the music, my mind began to travel to the little town of Bethlehem. I can see a man and a woman approaching the little town tired, hungry and a little scared. The woman had already started into labor and the man knew he had to quickly find a place for his wife to have the baby.

I can imagine Joseph desperately trying to find a place while his wife hoped he would be lucky soon. There was probably an older woman who either saw them or happened by the place where Mary was resting while Joseph searched. She knew she would have to help this poor frightened young woman. She probably helped Mary to the cave where she gave birth to our Lord.

Imagine with me for just a moment the place of our Lord's birth. It must have smelt of animal dung because this was where animals were kept. It was probably cold, dark and musty smelling. Joseph probably built a fire near the opening to help keep them warm and to keep away the wild animals.

I can also imagine the frustration that Joseph must have felt knowing he could not afford a doctor's care for his wife. I can also imagine his thoughts, "Oh God, look at the mess we're in now. Why couldn't we have been at home and had the baby like I had planned? Why did we have to come to Bethlehem?"

And then the baby's cry broke the winter's silence. The Christ child was born. He came into the world weak and helpless. He left the glory and wonder of heaven and became dependent on Mary and Joseph to provide everything for him. He had the riches of heaven, yet he was now a pauper.

Why? Why would he do it? He wanted everybody from any walk of life to be able to identify with him. He wanted us to know that the Father loved us. He wanted to be the perfect sacrifice so we could have fellowship and friendship with God.

Maybe my grandmother is right. We all need to slow down and have an old fashioned Christmas. We need a peaceful Christmas that allows time for reflection on the true meaning of the Christ child's birth in the little town of Bethlehem. As you complete the final preparations for Christmas, take some time to enjoy peace on earth and good will towards man.

Father, often at this time of year, our hearts and minds are so busy.
We have presents to buy, people to see, oh, so many things to do.
Please help us to slow down and to think about you.
Draw us close to your side,
help us to focus our dizzy eyes on the Christ child.
Help restore the peace in our hearts,
help us to share the "Good News."
Peace on earth,
Good Will toward men.
Father, restore our peace.
Open our eyes to
you.
Amen.

Christmas Gifts

Happy Birthday, Jesus! To celebrate Christmas my brother and his family are going to have a birthday party for Jesus. They will have a birthday cake with candles (not 2000 of them!) and they will sing happy birthday to Jesus. This, in my mind, is a special way to help his children understand the meaning of Christmas.

As I have been reflecting on the Christmas story this year, I have been thinking about the wise men and their presents. I find it very interesting that only one of the gospels, Matthew, mentions the three wise men. God put them in the Christmas story for a reason and I would like to offer a few thoughts on the matter.

The three wise men come from somewhere east of Bethlehem. The fact that they came on foot or by camel distances that would have taken months or possibly years to walk is truly amazing. Imagine the faith it would take to press on day after day. Also think about the miraculous star that God kept in the sky long enough for them to find Jesus.

Can you imagine the joy that must have filled their hearts once they arrived and saw Jesus? The Bible records that they fell down and worshipped Jesus. The Bible says nothing about them even bowing to Herod.

I can just see Mary and joseph coming back from town and finding three kings' caravans stopped at the place where they were staying. They were probably excited because they thought they might get to see a king. Imagine their reaction as they watched the kings falling prostrate in front of their child.

Think about how they must have felt receiving gifts from the kings. I bet Mary and Joseph were down to their last bit of money before these kings arrived. I can imagine Joseph's cry to the Lord, "God, where are we going to get money for our next meal? God, don't you even care about your own son?" Then God brings three kings Joseph's way. Isn't that just like God? We come to the end of our rope and then God pours out His extravagant love on us.

The extravagant gifts that God gave Mary and Joseph are interesting. The first mentioned was gold. A king deserved the best. The gold was to help provide for their daily physical needs. The scriptures promise that God will provide all your needs according to His riches in glory. God made sure Mary and Joseph had all the things they needed, not necessarily all the things they wanted.

The second gift was frankincense. This is a fragrant gum resin that was burned on an alter to the Lord. When it was burned it would provide a fragrant offering to God. Here again the wise men offered an expensive gift as a part of their worship of Jesus.

The last gift, myrrh, was a bittersweet gift. Myrrh was a fragrant perfume used in the burial process. This was a prophetic gift showing the purpose for Christ's birth. Jesus was born to die for mankind. I can envision Mary grabbing her baby up when this gift was offered. Like any other mother she would want to shield her baby from the pain that was ahead.

Jesus is the best gift we can all receive on Christmas. The gift of eternal life that He offers is free for anyone that will receive it. You do not deserve it, yet out of love the heavenly Father wants to give it to you. The cost to you is everything. But what do you have that can compare to the riches of eternal life with God the father?

I hope that you have received or will receive the best Christmas present ever. Merry Christmas from my heart to yours. May God lavishly pour out His love, grace, mercy and peace on your life and your home.

I resolve to...

In just a couple of days people everywhere will be celebrating the New Year. Where has the year gone? It was full of ups and downs, but you can't deny that it is almost over. The new year holds promise and the chance to start new and fresh. It's time to open the books to the new year and to see what fate has in store for us.

Many people over the next few days will be making resolutions about how the new year will be spent. People promise to change their bad habits and start new good habits. Two of the most popular new year's resolutions are to exercise and lose weight.

After we stuffed ourselves over the last month with holiday food it's time to take that extra weight off. Madison Avenue has a stockpile of commercials to help. There are shakes to drink, health clubs to join, and exercise equipment to purchase. All of these are designed to help firm up those loose muscles and get rid of the extra fat.

All the weight loss products promise that you will get instant results. Right. You spent a whole month putting the weight on and now you will take it off in one week? Our society seems to want instant results.

The other thing people resolve to work on is exercise. It's amazing to see the effort people put on in January to begin their exercise program. Many people get exercise equipment for Christmas. They start out completely committed to an exercise schedule. By mid-January the fire of commitment is waning to the pressures on our time. By the middle of February the exercise equipment has been moved from the family room back to a storage room where it waits to be sold in a summer yard sale. I think people have great intentions but when the going gets tough, people tend to bail out.

I often wonder if people make spiritual goals on New Years Eve. "I promise to read the entire Bible this year." "I will spend one hour praying every day." "I will stop sinning." Do people do the same thing with these resolutions as they do with resolutions to lose weight and exercise? Do they start out with great intentions and then forget the commitment when the road gets long and hard? Do people start out to read and pray more and by the middle of February quit?

I think God is pleased when He sees His children having a heartfelt desire to spend time with Him. I think He misses us when we forget and begin to do other things. What do you think God really wants? I think He, like any father, wants to spend time with His children. What God wants is some good quality time on a consistent basis.

I knew a man once who argued with me that he couldn't spend time with God because he was too busy. He reeled off a number of things that occupied his time. I have to admit that the things he named were very important things that demanded his time. I still believe he could have found some good quality time if he wanted to spend time with God.

I hold to the idea that God is more interested in quality than quantity. He is also more interested in consistency than spurts of big quantities of time then periods of no time at all.

The other thing I believe is that God does not give instant results. The Christian life requires a deep commitment for the long haul. If God is going to develop character in a man or woman He is going to take time to build it slowly and completely. That's another thing God wants, He wants people who will run the Christian life to the finish line.

As you consider your New Year's resolutions, may I challenge you to consider them carefully and choose something that you can stick to and accomplish. May I also encourage you to consider some spiritual goals that will cause you to walk closer with God. It will make you feel better about yourself and it will build character. Happy New Year everyone and may God Bless the year ahead. In and with His perfect peace.

Jesus as a Boy

Christmas has finally been tucked away in the boxes awaiting next year's arrival. The party hats, horns and noise makers are sleeping once again. The new year has arrived and it's time to start afresh. This is a new year with new perspectives, thoughts and opportunities.

As I begin this new year, I have been thinking about Jesus. To many of you that may not be a surprise. But I am not thinking about Jesus the prophet or Jesus the great teacher. I am thinking about Jesus, the young boy.

We know very little about Jesus before he was thirty. We know he was born in Bethlehem, lived for a short time in Egypt, and grew up in Nazareth. We also know that he was a carpenter. The only other events we know of his younger life were the two visits to the temple. The first visit occurred when he was just a few days old. During this visit Simeon and Anna both spoke great prophesies about him and his life. The second visit occurred when he was twelve. This was the trip when he stayed behind while his parents left to go home.

I do not believe that Jesus stayed to be rebellious. I think he got involved in the conversation and didn't realize his parents had left. Remember he was there for three days talking to the leaders. He was probably enjoying himself so much that he forgot about his parents.

Now switch roles. Imagine you were his parents. For three days you have been panicked looking for your child. Finally, you find him. Do you think you might be emotional? Would you speak calmly to him or would you yell at him? I can easily imagine a few choice words rolling out of my mouth. Would you have disciplined your child?

Disciplining Jesus is a very interesting thought. Mary and Joseph knew that Jesus was the Messiah. Do you think it would have been easy to correct or discipline him? Would you be afraid to discipline him because of what you thought God might do to you when you got to heaven? Do you think that God intended for Mary and Joseph to discipline His son?

Before I continue, I need to be sure you understand where I stand. I firmly believe that Jesus was perfect, completely free from sin. If that was true, why would Mary and Joseph need to discipline Jesus?

Jesus came into the world the same way we did. He was a baby that demanded a mother's attention and care. He was frail and if you dropped him he would cry. He did not come into the world saying "Hey Mom. Thanks for carrying me around for nine months. Sorry to be born and run, but I have a world to save."

Jesus was born like any human being needing love and discipline. Like any child, Jesus had to be taught to crawl, walk, talk, eat, how to work with daddy's tools, how to build fires, tend a garden and how to love and show compassion for those in need. As a school teacher, I know that even the best of students need to be disciplined occasionally. That does not imply that the students are morally wrong, but they must be taught how to behave. I think Jesus had to be taught right from wrong so he could learn to be obedient.

Jesus didn't enter the world completely knowledgeable. Jesus had to learn everything, even about God. I honestly believe that at four years old Jesus did not realize he was the Messiah. If he didn't know it when he was a child then he had to learn about it from God. How did Jesus learn it? The only way was to spend time with his Father in prayer.

How are we supposed to learn who we are in God? How are we supposed to learn our purpose in life? Through prayer and reading the word. I believe that if we spend time with God He will reveal His good plans for our lives.

I encourage you to seek the Lord for this coming year. If we seek Him and His presence in our lives we will learn more about Him and how to walk in His love and protection.

3 cute ones

+ 3 special ones

---

6 worth reading

*The following three columns were things I wrote when
I was attempting to get published for the first time.
They are not religious or particularly inspiring in nature,
but I thought they were humorous.
I hope you enjoy them.*

Andy Griffith

It's 5:30 and I can hear my favorite whistle. No, it's not the whistle to go home; it's the whistle for, "The Andy Griffith Show". When I hear that whistle I run to the frig and pour my ice tea, grab a snack and head for my favorite chair. I don't know about you, but I just love "The Andy Griffith Show". I'm not alone with my love affair, because more Americans are watching than ever before and have caused it to rise to new levels of popularity.

Why? The reasons are as diverse as the people watching the show. The reasons I enjoy the show are too numerous for one column, but let's talk about a few of them. First, could you imagine calling the police today and seeing the officer walk in your home without a gun? I would be more scared after he or she arrived than before. But not Andy. There were only a few shows where you actually see Andy use a gun. Most of those involve him doing some skeet shooting. I think one reason so many people like his show is the fact that there were no violent crimes. If you like violence, turn on the news; you'll see plenty. I prefer the escapism that Andy provides from our violent world.

Next, could you imagine running into a police station today to report a crime and finding the sheriff in there playing a guitar and singing? We would vote him out of office so fast his head would spin. Can you imagine your doctor coming out to have a few songs with the patients in the waiting room before the examination? You and I live in such a fast-paced world we would probably get up and walk right out of that office. What a shame.

I think we are so busy in our career-oriented world that we fail to slow down and smell the roses or relax on our porches after a delicious evening meal. We are always in such a rush to get here and there that we fail to appreciate the smaller things in life, maybe life itself. For one half hour a day we can set our busy schedules aside and relax with some old friends who know how to have good clean fun with nobody getting hurt. Andy Griffith is the kind of show that we can all laugh at, identify with, and possible envy their slow paced, relaxed, carefree lives. While you and I are bogged down in the many cares of life these people seem to sail right through it.

Why is Andy popular? Who wouldn't love to sit down to one of Aunt Bee's home cooked meals? Or have an honest mechanic like Goober or Gomer work on your car? Or have Helen Crump teach your children? Or have Floyd bend your ear while he cut your hair for only 50 cents? Or who in their right mind wouldn't want to live in a town where you felt completely safe, like Mayberry? Oh, excuse me, but I hear that familiar whistle. Guess what? It's the one with Aunt Bee's pickles. I think I'll eat a pickle with my tea today.

Cleaning

I am a school teacher and there are a few happier people than teachers when summer vacation finally arrives. We are finally free to do whatever we want for two very short months. One of the many things that gets done around my house is spring cleaning. Spring cleaning is worse for me and my wife because we both have a tendency to be pack rats (ie. we never throw anything away).

Every summer arrives with the same difficult challenges; what to keep and what to throw away. It is amazing to see how much "stuff" accumulates over a ten month period. There are bows from Christmas, gifts that were never used, seeds from last year's garden, clothes that don't fit anymore, dead flowers that we just couldn't bear to throw out, deflated mylar balloons and old newspapers that we were saving for some reason or another. Then there are those numerous craft projects that we promised ourselves we would work on while we watched TV.

Now is the time to begin going through all that "stuff" and making the difficult decisions about whether to keep it or not. Here lies my second problem... remember, I am a pack rat. Pack rats keep everything because someday it might be of some use. I have thrown stuff out before only to discover days later that I needed the very thing I threw out to solve some problem. So what do I do?

My dad is a wise man so I decided to call him. Dad is facing a similar problem as he is to be married again after living alone for a number of years. I know he has accumulated a whole bunch of "stuff" or junk. (Note: Other people's "stuff" is "junk" to you and me.) As we began our conversation I noticed some noise in the background. Dad told me it was his fiancée cleaning out all his "stuff" for a garage sale that she was going to have. "That's not fair," I thought, "She is doing all the dirty work." A garage sale, however, is a good idea if your stuff is worth selling. You see, people like to look through your "junk" to see if they can find some more "stuff" for themselves. I decided not to have a garage sale because...oh yeah, I don't have a garage.

Next I decided to call my brother. My brother has the idea if you haven't used your "stuff" in the last year then throw it out (either Good Will or the garbage whichever is more appropriate). That would be a great idea if we were talking about lawn mowers and hedge clippers which I would gladly not use for one year so I could throw them out. But what about a pair of scissors that work fine but have one of the tips broken off? Or that perfectly good shirt that needs a button? Or the pants that would fit perfectly if you lost a couple pounds? I sat around and used my questionable "stuff" that day so that his rule would not apply.

What to do? What to do? Most teachers just go to the beach once summer finally arrives. My wife and I are doomed to look through all this "stuff" and decide whether to keep it or throw it out. I have a great idea! Since we hardly ever throw anything away and it's not spring any more, let's forget spring cleaning and go to the beach. Wow, that was the easiest "spring cleaning" I have ever done. Grab your swimsuit honey, we are heading for the beach.

WALMART vs. KMART

I live just outside of Salisbury and I work at North Stanly High School which is close to Albemarle. There is a war going on in these two towns. It is not a war fought with guns, tanks and bombs. This is a very different type of war that involves two competitive parties that would go to almost any length to destroy each other. The parties use more strategies and tactics than were used in Desert Storm. The battle is reminiscent of Macy's and Gimble's in the beginning of *Miracle on Thirty-Fourth Street*. The enemies of today's showdown are Walmart and Kmart.

I don't have a personal favorite. Both stores provide basically the same types of products and a nice environment in which to shop. They both employ friendly people who will try to help you find what you need. So what are they fighting over? The customer. They both want to be number one.

I have to admit I like it. I even enjoy having a little fun while I shop at these stores. For example, if I am shopping at Walmart and I noticed that their price is higher than Kmart, I take great pleasure in letting them now.

"Did you find what you were looking for, sir?" the salesperson asks.

"Yeah, but I can't believe this price." I say in an agitated way.

"What do you mean?"

"I can get the same thing at Kmart for three dollars less." The reaction of the salesperson is worth a million dollars. It's like they can't believe you would entertain such a thought. I have to walk out of the store empty handed, shaking my head to add some extra emphasis. I know it's wrong, but I love doing that.

However, there is one issue I would like to address that does get under my skin. As I have already stated, I work and live in different towns. I sometimes feel guilty taking all my money out of town, so I make an extra effort to spend my money in the town where I work. If I read a Kmart or Walmart ad in the comfort of my home than I expect that any of the stores ought to have the same sales. They are both national chains but they use localized sales promotions and circulars. In their defense, I have been told that if I bring the ad with me when I shop, they will honor the price. Great, I can hardly remember all the things I need when I get there, now I have to remember to bring the ad too! Oh well, maybe it's their way of getting back at me.

The bottom line about these two businesses going head to head in competition is that you and I (the customer) will get the benefits. We get lower prices and better service. Believe me, many other businesses could learn from the courtesy and friendliness that these two fine chains are offering.

"Attention, Kmart shoppers, there is a blue light special in aisle thirteen." This could be a good deal or it could be one of their tactics to get you to buy something. The only way to be sure is to go to Walmart and check .....fast!

The Youth Breakfast & Rhoda

I was asked to speak at a youth breakfast in Albemarle. When I was approached I was told that there would be three teachers to address the students the morning I spoke. I prayed long and hard about the opportunity and felt in my spirit God was calling me to speak, so I agreed to do it.

About a week or two before the big day I found out that a student was going to speak instead of a teacher from one of the schools. I didn't like the sound of that. Why? Often students will tell others that God is love and that everybody is going to heaven and there is no hell. They often speak in flowery terms and giggle and laugh a lot. I know that this comes from nervousness, but I was afraid that the truth would be compromised by the student speaker. I wanted out but felt it would be wrong to bow out at that late date. You can bet I complained a lot in God's ear and did not listen to His heart.

I determined, in my own mind, that I should speak last so I could fix whatever this student had messed up. I met the woman in charge and she confirmed the order of speakers, putting me in the middle. I engaged in some small talk waiting for the perfect moment to ask her to let me speak last. The moment came and just as I was about to open my mouth I heard in my spirit, "Be still and know that I am God."

I excused myself from the woman and found a quiet place where I might enquire more of the Lord. I asked him to explain. He said simply that he had called me to speak to the youth that morning, but that he had also called the other speakers too. He reminded me that he was a big enough God to know the order of the speakers and to get the order that he desired. He told me not to tamper with what he had done. Then he reminded me that He loved me. His rebuke was straightforward and given in love. I was able to accept it and to go wait my turn to speak.

The speaker before me was good. She laid a firm foundation of the gospel of Jesus Christ. The word was plain and clear and right from her heart. I noticed the students were not listening as closely as I had hoped. Then the Lord opened my mouth and I continued to lay the foundation of Jesus as the only answer for their generation. When I finished I began to pray for the next young lady as she took the platform.

Rhoda took the microphone and started to share the story of her life right from her heart. You could have heard a pin drop anywhere in that room. She had their complete attention. They were on the edge of their seats and so was I. My mouth hung open as I listened to her share her testimony of Jesus' love and mercy. The radiance of Jesus' love filled her voice and shone around her face.

She was the crown jewel that morning. When I got up to leave I knew God was in control. I would have hated to have followed her. She was excellent, spellbinding. The whole way back to school in the car I thanked the Lord over and over for helping me keep my big mouth shut. I also thanked him for the opportunity to speak and for filling my mouth with His words.

That afternoon I found Rhoda and talked to her for about forty-five minutes. Her testimony is unbelievable. Jesus has been faithful to her over and over again.

When I drove home that evening I couldn't stop thinking how the love and the power of Jesus was bursting through her eyes. There was fire in her eyes that was not in mine. I tried to tell myself that I was tired from work and everything but it just wouldn't settle. Then I convinced myself that the fire was burning so strong in her eyes because she had spoken that morning. I decided I would test that theory in a few days.

A few days later I looked Rhoda up and asked her a question. When I got her aside I asked her how she was doing, you know the way you always ask not really meaning it. She looked at me and said, "I'm great!" The fire in her eyes was brighter than ever. When I drove home that night I thought about that fire in her eyes even more. I had fire like that once, where was my fire? I looked in the rear view mirror and saw a smoldering wick. "Where's the fire, Lord?" I cried out.

Every time after that whenever I saw Rhoda in the hall at school the fire burst through her eyes. I found that challenging and it caused me to start seeking the Lord to restore my fire. It didn't take long before the Lord met me and rekindled my fire. To show the degree to which God restored my fire, one of my classes commented that I had changed. I asked them what they meant and they said that something was different about me. They didn't know what it was but they liked the change they saw. They were seeing Jesus in me.

Fire in the eyes. Jesus said we would look different to the world. He told us to let our light shine before men that they might see our good deeds and glorify our Father in heaven. Jesus said we are the salt of the earth. We are what preserves this world. I encourage you to look into the mirror and examine your fire. Does your fire light the way to Jesus Christ? Does your fire challenge those around you to believe in Jesus? Are you a beacon to the lost in this world? If you feel you need your fire to be rekindled, I encourage you to seek the Lord and the fire of His spirit will fill you.

The "Covered" Gourd of Great Price

A while back a friend invited my wife and I to dinner. It is nice to get together with friends and sit down to a good meal. The fellowship is almost equally important to me. The fellowship at this friend's house was sweet.

We got the tour of the kitchen, living room, dining room and den. They have a beautiful, well-decorated home. It has a very homey atmosphere. The other thing I felt, besides very welcome, was a very laid back relaxed feeling. It was the kind of home that made you feel good, a place where the peace of Christ was present.

While in the kitchen, I noticed a very unusual gourd hanging in the kitchen. It caught my eye because it had been lovingly covered with small pieces of fabric. I was so intrigued I just had to ask about it. The host explained that she used scrap cloth. Some of the scraps came from her favorite maternity dress that she wore while expecting her first child. Some of the other pieces came from old clothes that her children had outgrown. Still other pieces came from fabric she used to make Christmas ornaments.

She said there was a story that went with the gourd if I was interested. Naturally, I was. She said that she covered the gourd many years ago and that at some unknown point in time she lost possession of it. How, she doesn't know. She thinks it could have gotten lost in a move or mistakenly put out with the garbage while cleaning out the basement. Anyway, she said that she had missed it over the years mainly because of its sentimental value.

One day, years later, she said she was driving through town and she saw it sitting at someone's yard sale! She stopped the van and ran over to get it. She explained to the person the value it held for her and offered the people selling it double the price. The lady selling it told her she could just have it. She took it home and carefully cleaned off all the dirt that had accumulated during its absence. Now it hangs proudly in her kitchen.

I watched my friend as she caressed the outside of the gourd. She had a twinkle in her eye. It was obvious that the gourd was very valuable to her. I could see it in her face all the memories of her children flooding her mind as she held the gourd.

This story brought several parables to life for me. The first was the pearl of great price. If you remember in the parable Jesus told that a merchant finds a very expensive pearl and then goes and sells everything he has to buy it. My friend was willing to pay double the price for her gourd. How many of us have given up everything to follow Jesus? Have we decided to live entirely for God's kingdom or are we still trying to straddle the fence and live in both the kingdoms?

The other parable that comes to mind is the parable of the lost coin. If you remember this is the one where the woman loses a coin and searches diligently for it. When she finds it she rejoices and calls friends and neighbors and tells them that she has found it. I am sure my friend tells the story of finding the gourd often.

In the same way the scriptures say that heaven rejoices over one sinner who repents. Do you remember when you committed your life to the Lord? Didn't you want to tell everybody about the new life that you found?

My friend told me that she asked the lady who had the gourd where she had gotten it. She said she bought it at another yard sale. There is no telling where that gourd had been while it was missing from my friend's house. That didn't matter to my friend because that gourd was still as valuable to her as the day she made it. That is just like Jesus. He buys us and covers us with His valuable blood. Once we become a child of God we never lose our value in God's eyes. It doesn't matter where we have been or what we have done, we are still exceedingly valuable to God.

I can imagine the day when our Father sends Jesus to get us. Jesus will be riding in His chariot and when He sees us He will jump out of His chariot to get us. He will take us before the Father and explain to the Father how valuable we are and how much He loves us. Then Jesus will tell the Father, "I paid the highest price for this child. I bought this child with my blood." Then Jesus will bring us into heaven, as His priceless treasure.

We often put ourselves down and we don't think we are very valuable to God. We have to remember that God allowed His one and only Son to die so we could spend eternity with Him. There is a price for sin and Jesus paid that price in full. There is nothing we can do to buy or earn our way into heaven. Salvation is a free gift from God.

I encourage you to wash yourself in the blood of Christ. Receive God's mercy and forgiveness again. Clothe yourself with His robes of righteousness. You are exceedingly valuable to God and He loves you without measure. You are like that gourd to my friend. You are a valuable treasure to God.

And God Wept

I wrote this column right after the Oklahoma City bombing.
It could have been written after 9/11 or so many other tragedies.
It was one of the most inspired things I have ever written.
It touched many lives and I felt it belonged in this book. I hope
it blesses you like it has so many others.

I imagine Saint Peter walked into God's throne room last Wednesday to talk to God about a problem at the Pearly Gates.
"God, could I talk to you for a minute?"
"Peter! It's great to see you. How can I help?"
"I came because there seems to be a little problem in the paperwork. A large group has arrived ahead of schedule."
"Are they from Oklahoma City?" Peter nodded. "Yeah, there was an unexpected change of plans. I'm sorry, I forgot to send word of the changes." God said wiping away a tear.
"What happened?" Peter asked.
"Do you remember what happened a long time ago with Job and his family?" Peter nodded. "Well," God continued with a sigh, "Satan came up here about a week ago. He had this grand scheme on how he was going to destroy the faith of the people of Oklahoma through terrorism. He had to ask permission because his plan involved taking human lives. I didn't like the plan but I was convinced that the people would pull together and faith would triumph."
"But why did you approve the plan?"
"I've been sending warning after warning to America that they must turn from their sinful ways, but they don't seem to be listening. I've sent terrible earthquakes, droughts, floods and huge storms. It seems to get their attention for a moment or two and then they return to their sinful ways. I desperately want fellowship with them but they seem too busy to spend time with me. They don't understand that their actions are deciding eternity.
"They also don't understand the forces that affect their world. Satan is alive and he is intent on doing wicked and evil things. There is a spiritual battle going on around them every day. When

disasters like this occur they turn to me with questions of "Why?" They don't understand that Satan is the author of evil deeds. Satan will continue to do evil things. In fact, as we draw closer to the end of their time his evil deeds and persecution will increase.

"Well, Satan's deed is done." God said. "Get word to the Christians around the world to begin praying for the people of Oklahoma City. Send a battalion of angels and ministering spirits to comfort and encourage the people of the city. Rally the necessary ingredients to build hope in the people. Send an assault on the barriers that keep people apart, such as pride, racism and wealth. Set the ground work for unity. Maybe then they will be able to pull through this tragedy."

"Yes Lord, I will take care of all that right away. We still have one more problem," Peter said. "We divided the new arrivals into three groups. The first group is those needing processing into heaven, which we have begun. The second group is those being processed for hell. We have also begun their paperwork. My question is what to do with this third group. These are people who attend church occasionally. They never made a commitment to your Son. Our records show that if they had lived a full life they probably would have made the commitment to Christ. What should we do with this group?"

"Peter, what are the requirements to get into heaven?"

"People must confess with their lips that Jesus is Lord and they must believe that you raised him from the dead."

"What is the status on this group of people?"

"Lord, they haven't done that yet. But God, everybody down in processing believes they would have done it eventually."

"Peter, if they have been in church on and off throughout their lives then I have been wooing them. They have heard the word and rejected it. It was their choice. No one is guaranteed tomorrow, Peter. There are plenty of people walking the earth today who have put the most important decision of their lives on hold. There is a price, and in this case, a heavy price for putting off that decision."

Peter hung his head and he started to leave. "Please close the door as you leave." God called out. "I would like a few minutes alone." When Peter had closed the door and left, God fell to heaven's floor and He wept.

Saying Good-bye

Everything is typed and ready to go to press. All I have left to do is copy the files over to finish the final disk to take to the printer. This book has required more effort than I thought possible. One minute I am excited, the next I am down. My stomach is full of butterflies and my feet are stone cold. I am guessing and hoping all these things are normal. The time has arrived to release my book and see if it flies, hovers or crashes.

Before I finish, I decided I might offer a few parting thoughts. Let me begin by saying, this book is the beginning of a new adventure for me. It is a journey of faith. Writing and self-publishing this book has put my faith to the test. I have to trust the Lord as He leads me. I was talking to a friend recently about a few printing questions that I had to make, when she asked me, "You believe the Lord told you to write the book, don't you?" I paused and thought about her question. "That requires faith," I thought. The answer was still, "Yes."

Faith is not something you can touch or feel. Faith is just there deep down inside you. When God calls us to do something it requires faith on our part. There will be Goliaths and Jerichos that will need to be conquered. They are things we can never defeat on our own, they require faith. We have to trust God that He will help us to conquer the things that lay between us and our promised land. Faith requires us to believe and to trust the Lord. But in order to enter our promised land we have to be loyal to God, that is a part of faith too.

Another closing thought deals with spending time with the Lord. Those of you who are regular readers will know that I write about that topic every chance I get. The only sure-fire way to grow in Christ is to spend time with Him. You know the old expression, "We become what our friends are." If you are hanging out with Jesus on a regular basis, you will become more like Him. That's our goal in this life, to become more like Christ.

The past few weeks I have been working as hard as I could to finish this book. I want it to be ready for Christmas. I have used every spare moment to complete the manuscript. This past weekend was my final deadline. It had to be done by Monday, or it wouldn't be ready for Christmas. I worked harder than I believed possible to finish. In the process, I slid on spending time with my Father. I was so busy doing what I know He has called me to do, I wasn't spending uninterrupted time with Him. Oh, He got a prayer here and a prayer there, just not good quality time.

I was getting ready to work on this ending piece, when I felt a nudge, "Turn the computer off. Come spend some time with me." I love being out working in the yard. (I know my mother and father won't believe that, because I avoided yard work like the flu when I was growing up.) Now that I am an adult, with my own yard, I love to be outside working in it.

I turned the computer off and headed outside. It was a beautiful day. There was plenty of work waiting for me outside, so I jumped in. As I began to work, I began to pray. I felt the Lord's presence very strongly. I felt His love for me. I have been learning a lot about grace recently. I can't adequately express in words what grace is to me, probably because I am learning more about it even as I write these words. Anyway, I felt His grace and His love as I worked in the yard. I also felt a profound sense of peace. It's the kind of peace that reaches inside you and transforms you.

His spirit washed me and refreshed my soul. When I finished the work outside, I felt great. God wants to spend time with each of us every day. He desires intimacy with His children. You know those moments when your parents hold you in their arms and you know that everything will turn out OK? That's what God wants with us, His children. He desires to hold us in His arms so we can know that everything is under His control and it will work out.

I encourage you to find that time to spend with your Father. He loves you with the perfect love that never ends, and doesn't change because of your behavior. Come to Jesus and allow Him to take all those burdens off your life. Come to Jesus and find your purpose and your place in life. You are a child of your Father in Heaven, and He loves you without measure. Spend time with Him every day and you will find grace, faith, hope and love.

One final thought before I say good-bye. My Father in Heaven is not a God of rules. The God that I serve does not sit in heaven and list all the good things I do and all the bad things I do. God's love for us has nothing to do with obeying a bunch of rules. God loves us as His children. Our relationship is with a living being.

When I sin, God isn't sitting in heaven saying, "Doug just blew it again. But, in his favor, that was a little rule. He only gets a little penalty for that one." Then a few hours later, or seconds, depending on the situation: "Ooopps, Doug blew that one big time. Make a note of that. He will have to be punished big time for that one." That is not the way my Father is, or the way He treats me. God knows you and I are going to fail. He already knows that we will sin, so he provided a way for us to continue our relationship. He sent His Son to take away our sins. God loves us, even though we are sinners. He doesn't keep track of our sins because Jesus has cleansed us from them.

Now Satan and our minds are different stories. When Satan tries to bring guilt and condemnation on us, we have to remember Jesus took those away too when He died on the cross. When our minds remind us of our sins, we have to remind our minds that we have been washed in the blood of Christ. Jesus' blood cleansed us of our sins. Remember, our Father does not keep record of sins, as long as we confess them, we are forgiven and our sin is forgotten.

With those three things shared, it's time to say, "Good-bye." I want you to know that you are holding my dream in your hands. Writing a book has always been a dream of mine. Today, you are holding the finished product. Someone very special told me that when God gives you an assignment, you must give it your best effort then put it back into His hands. It's up to Him at that point. He can do with it as He pleases. So, back to God it goes.

I have tried to figure out how I should say, "Good-bye," but I don't have a clue. I have considered famous people's signature sign offs, such as; Garrison Keillor, Paul Harvey, Walter Cronkite, or Paul from the scriptures. I was even planning to do a parody of their closings, substituting my own words for your entertainment. The problem with that was it seemed flashy and it would be copying someone else's work.

The best way to end my book, is not to say, "Good-bye" at all. I hope this is only the beginning of what is to come. I have lots of ideas for books running around in my head; I just have to find the time to write them. At the very least I hope to write another similar book. First, however, I need a break from the work. I also have some lost time to make up with my wife.

For my loyal readers, I will see you next week in the paper. For those who get my columns through email or my website, I'll see you the next time I post or send. For those of you who have just met me for the first time in this book, I hope to see you again, when my next book comes out. To all of you, I thank you for your support and encouragement. You will never know how much your words of encouragement mean. Thank you again.

Don't forget to share your encouraging thoughts with others! God Bless You, and may His peace surround you.

Mercy
Grace
Faith
Hope
Love
In the Peace of Christ,
Doug

I have two novels that are for sale at Amazon or you can purchase them directly from me. I am including chapter one from both books so you can taste the novels before you buy them. I hope you enjoy them.... Here is Chapter 1 from *The Bluebird Café*...

The Bluebird Café

Chapter 1

It was 6:15 in the morning when Jenny's key slid into the lock of the Bluebird Cafe. The Bluebird had been at this location in Virginia Beach for almost fifty years. It had been remodeled several times over the years, yet it still stood strong as a testament to the craftsmen who built it. It had survived hurricanes, powerful spring storms and winter's cold blasts. Even the explosive population growth had done little to ruin the warmth of the little cafe.

The counter was the original, but the stools had been upgraded fifteen years ago. The previous owner had expanded the cafe by adding booths along the front and two sides. Customers enjoyed watching the ocean from the side booths, so those seats always filled up first.

Behind the main counter on the right hand side was the grill, which Jenny had enlarged when she bought the cafe. From the grill the cook could easily interact with the customers who sat at the counter. On the left sat the coffee machines, soda dispenser, glass-front refrigerator and a large menu that hung on the back wall. None of the owners of the Bluebird had ever bothered to print a menu because most of the customers, including the vacationers, were regulars and they knew what they wanted.

Jenny pushed the door open and turned on the lights. Within a few minutes, the smell of freshly brewed coffee filled the air. Jenny was singing softly as she began the morning ritual of preparing for the breakfast crowd. The sound of the local morning show disc jockeys crackled from the old radio which sat atop the refrigerator. In between their jokes and bantering, country music played from the old speaker.

Jenny was thirty years old (she bought the Bluebird when she was twenty-five). Jenny had long sandy blond hair which she kept tied up under her hat while she was at work. Her blue-green eyes could melt butter with their warmth and tenderness. Her skin seemed to be eternally tanned and her figure was definitely feminine. Jenny had to work to keep her figure, but she often wondered why she put so much effort into it.

Jenny's morning routine always included setting a place for her "early bird special," Uncle Charlie. Uncle Charlie was not really Jenny's uncle. He was, in fact, the previous owner of the Bluebird Cafe. He had sold Jenny the cafe five years ago, but he never missed his morning breakfast at the ever-so-familiar counter.

Jenny looked out the window and saw the headlights make their usual turn into the paved parking lot. She continued about her business getting things ready to open. Five minutes later Jenny realized that Uncle Charlie hadn't yet come in. She came up front to look for him and found him just outside the front door. He was talking to someone who looked like he hadn't had a shower in several days.

Jenny smiled because she knew in a few hours that rough-looking man would be showered and sitting in the corner booth eating breakfast provided by Uncle Charlie. Oh, he would never admit to buying his meal. He would say that he was bringing the man's money up to the cash register because he was too embarrassed. She knew the routine by now, and she just smiled and went along.

"Ding, Ding." The bell over the door rang as Uncle Charlie came in to take his spot at the end of the counter. At slightly less than six feet tall, he was a well-balanced man. Although Uncle Charlie was in his seventies, one would never know it. Nothing seemed to slow him down except a person in need. His hair was white and thin on top. He wore glasses but they only enhanced his deep blue eyes. You would never find Uncle Charlie without his trademark pipe. He loved a smoke after each meal. But the pipe, often unlit, never seemed to be far from the corner of his mouth. He smoked a sweet smelling tobacco that even Jenny had to admit she liked. Jenny rarely allowed anyone to smoke in the Bluebird, except Uncle Charlie.

"Good morning, Uncle Charlie!" Jenny's greeting rang out from the backroom. "Take your seat and I'll be right out."

Uncle Charlie fixed himself a cup of coffee and headed for his favorite seat. He opened the paper and was taking his first sip of coffee when Jenny asked, "The usual: two eggs, two link sausage and three pancakes?" Uncle Charlie nodded and continued to scan the front page of the paper.

"It's fixing to be a hot one out there," he said when Jenny brought him his order. "They say it might break a hundred today."

"I just hope that old air conditioner won't break down and leave us out in the cold. Or melting in the heat, I should say." The old air conditioner had been hanging in its place for nearly twenty years. Even after all those years of service, it still chugged along faithfully. Jenny smiled, as she refilled his coffee cup. "Anything worth worrying about in those headlines," she asked, pointing to the paper.

"Nah, just the usual. Hey, did you see the Braves game last night?"

"No, I'm afraid not. I had a date last night," she said as Uncle Charlie's eyes got big. "But don't you worry, he was a dud just like the rest of them. Uncle Charlie, why is it that a man thinks you owe him something if he takes you to a dinner and a movie?"

"They're not all like that, honey. You've got to keep your eyes open and you'll find the right one for you."

"It's not that I haven't been around the block a few times. I actually enjoy a man's company for the evening. I just don't like it when they expect it, that's all."

"I understand," Uncle Charlie said, with a thoughtful pause. "Hey, what about the police officer, Mike, that has lunch in here three times a week? I've seen him make eyes at you."

"Get out of here. That man has never made no 'eyes' at me. I know better. Besides what would a cop want with someone like me?"

"You have a lot to offer! You're young, you've got a good head on your shoulders, you've got a nice figure and you own your own business. You are an honest, responsible, decent and caring business owner. I know plenty of men who would love to go out with you. Just keep those eyes open 'cause you never know who God might bring your way."

"Where are all the guys like you, Uncle Charlie?"

"In rest homes or graveyards," he said, and they both laughed. "But don't you give up. I know there's a decent guy out there just waiting to find someone as nice as you." She smiled at the thought and shook her head. "Besides, you better be careful or I might ask you out," he said, with a smile. Jenny just shook her head as she got back to work preparing for the morning rush. Uncle Charlie went back to reading his paper.

Before long the place was hopping with the morning crowd. Uncle Charlie's old buddies were sitting with him talking sports. Every once in a while the group would erupt in laughter. Most of the other customers at the Bluebird were regulars; and if they didn't speak to Uncle Charlie, Uncle Charlie spoke to them.

As quickly as the breakfast crowd arrived, they were gone. Uncle Charlie's old buddies broke up their "meeting" and headed for home. Uncle Charlie moved from his favorite seat to the corner booth. The rough-looking man who was talking to Uncle Charlie earlier that morning was seated at the booth eating the breakfast Uncle Charlie bought him. Jenny smiled as she watched. She knew Uncle Charlie was encouraging him not to give up on life. She could almost see him planting seeds of hope in the dejected man's soul.

When the fellow had finished his meal, he and Uncle Charlie sat and talked for almost two hours. Jenny saw Uncle Charlie light his pipe several times during their conversation. The smoke rose from his pipe like incense. When they were finally finished, Uncle Charlie came to the register.

"He gave me this to pay for his meal," Uncle Charlie said as he handed her a ten. Jenny just smiled because she knew better. She made the change and said,

"Tell your friend 'Good luck'."

"Oh, I think he'll be fine. He just needs a few breaks and things will turn themselves right around. I have high hopes for this one." Uncle Charlie headed back to the table and helped the stranger collect his things and they headed out the door together. They stood out by Uncle Charlie's old Chevy Luv truck talking for about half an hour before they parted.

Uncle Charlie came back into the cafe, which was now deserted. After pouring himself another cup of coffee, he took up residence at his usual spot. He lit his pipe and leaned back in his chair. Jenny poured herself a cup of coffee and sat down next to Uncle Charlie. The morning rush was over and there would only be an hour break before the lunch crowd would start coming in. It was just long enough for her to sit and talk to Uncle Charlie.

"You think you helped that fellow out?" Jenny asked, as she took a sip of her coffee.

"Yeah, I think so," Uncle Charlie said, taking a puff on his pipe.

"You don't sound very confident."

"He lost his wife about a month ago and he just lost his job last week. His boss said he hadn't been performing up to expectations." Uncle Charlie stopped. Then he said, "How can they let a man go who is obviously still suffering over the loss of his wife?"

"Profit, Uncle Charlie. Profit!" she exclaimed.

"Where is their compassion?" he asked.

"It doesn't fit onto the bottom line. If a man is not productive, you let him go. It's as simple as that." she said matter-of-factly.

"But he made the company lots of money over the years. Couldn't they give him a chance to get over the loss of his wife? That doesn't happen overnight, you know." Jenny could tell that this fellow's story had gotten to Uncle Charlie more than the usual "visitor," as he called them.

"I think I'll call that company and give them a piece of my mind," he said, as he pounded the counter.

"Now, Uncle Charlie, get a hold of yourself. You can't fix all the problems in this world and you know it. I know this one may seem unfair to you but you've got to let it go. You can't go out there and fight battles for everybody else. Sometimes you have to let people fight their own battles."

This didn't sit well with Uncle Charlie. But as he looked into Jenny's eyes, he realized she was right. She helped to keep him on the right path. Jenny and Uncle Charlie sat quietly for a little while. Uncle Charlie drank some coffee and took a few puffs on his pipe.

They started to talk about the Braves game from the previous night. Uncle Charlie gave Jenny an inning-by-inning commentary. Jenny listened patiently to her dear old friend. After he recounted the Braves victory, Jenny finished her coffee and started preparing for lunch. Uncle Charlie picked up the paper and resumed reading.

Here is Chapter one from *Revenge at the Bluebird Café*...

Revenge at the Bluebird Café

Chapter One

Robb Thomas turned left onto Atlantic Avenue in Virginia Beach. Atlantic Avenue, known as "the strip" to locals, was lined with oceanfront hotels. He drove past the statue of Poseidon, which served to welcome weary travelers to the haven of the seashore. He pulled his car into the parking lot of the Cavalier Hotel. The Cavalier was located at the end of the hotel strip. Next to it began a residential zone, so its location gave a sense of peace and quiet while still being connected to all the beach has to offer.

He checked into his room on the twelfth floor for a two week stay. He ordered a bottle of the best champagne and poured himself a glass while he sat on his oceanfront balcony. Robb surveyed the beach, taking in all the beautifully tanned women and the occasional stark white tourist who filled the scene before him.

Robb drained his second glass of champagne and retreated to the coolness of his room, which was plush and oversized. A basket of fresh fruit waited to be raided on the table near the window. The room held a king-sized bed on the far wall and an intimate sitting area near the sliding glass doors that led to the balcony. The fifty-inch flat screen TV hung on the wall above the sitting area.

He poured himself a third glass of champagne and set it on the bedside table. He pulled out his notepad from his leather briefcase and looked over his notes again. He chuckled to himself feeling excessively proud of what he had accomplished on such short order. He picked up the phone and placed a call. Robb was still chuckling when the man at the other end answered,

"Hello, Boss. This is Robb. Reconnaissance mission complete."

"What?" came the surprised voice at the other end. "You only left this morning. How can your reconnaissance be complete?"

"Boss, I went to the old man's funeral. I couldn't have gotten better information if I had requested it from the local library."

"Be careful who you're calling 'old man' there, my boy. Now, I would like to hear some details, something to substantiate your claims."

"The preacher didn't give the regular eulogy at his funeral. He talked for a few minutes, but he also invited the mourners to share the impact the old man... uhhh... the guest of honor had on their lives. Many people stood up, introduced themselves, and then told how he had helped them," he said, laughing excitedly.

"No wonder I hear champagne bubbling in the background," he said. "I assume you have also started to make a plan of action for us."

"I picked up the local paper, *The Virginian-Pilot*, and plan to contact a real estate agent in the morning. I'll find us a nice executive suite and have the office set up within a week."

"Been rethinking that since you left this morning. I would like you to set up our office away from the beachfront. I pulled up a map on Google. Look out in the Kempsville area. Witchduck Road, Kempsville Road, Princess Anne Road and Providence Road. See if you can find a nice office space in that area. We will need more than one office set up to do the job right; so let's start with one in a more discreet location."

"Yes sir," he said, jotting himself a few notes on a legal pad.

"Now, give me some of those 'details' you picked up at the funeral."

"The toughest client will be a local real estate company, King Realty. The owner has a strong hold on the market. He sells in the Kings Grant, Cavalier Golf Club, Bird Neck area; most of his stuff is upscale, located on either golf courses or waterfront properties."

"Do you think we can take him down through established businesses?"

"No, I think we're going to have to open our own office. I'll study the market and see if we can buy anyone out. I've got a feeling it would be easier to build from the ground up on that one."

"You get started on that immediately. I want King Realty out of business within six months or at the outside a year."

"That could be a stretch, but we'll get to work on it."

"We've got some slick salespeople in Chicago, New York and LA; don't hesitate to call in some of the troops. Why don't we put a lawyer and a finance officer in that office? Make the real estate company one-stop shopping; you know, streamline the operation. I'm not interested in profit on this venture, just crushing the enemy."

"Gotcha, Boss. Next, you've got the girl and the Bluebird."

"Leave her to me. I have special plans for her."

"Check." Robb looked up from his notes to see a house finch land on his balcony and grab a peanut that had escaped the maid's cleaning. He chirped his victory as he flew away with it in his beak. Focusing on his notes again, "There's a doctor; he's a heart specialist. Then you got a banker, a branch manager in one of the local offices. And we can't forget the preacher. All these I imagine have pretty clean slates, you know, no skeletons in closets."

"Don't assume that. Everyone has things that they want to keep secret. You know, what we need there is a reporter who can dish up a good scoop on those three."

Robb popped on the big screen TV and hit the mute button. He flipped over to ESPN Sports and watched as he continued. "I guess we could try and find someone to trash these guys' reputations."

"Not just someone," the Boss said thoughtfully, "how about Eve?"

"You want to bring Eve in on this one?"

"I told you we are going to spare no expense to destroy all the good work this old man did. I want these people to turn their backs on God. We're bigger and we're more powerful than any old god they can dream up."

The highlights showed a player scoring a grand slam. He missed the hit but managed to see the player jump into the welcoming party at home plate. "I'll call Eve in the morning," he said, wishing he had seen the hit.

"Is the editor of the paper a male or female?"

"Uh, give me second," he said reaching for the paper and flipping to the second page, "yeah it's a male."

"Then Eve is our man, or should I say woman? Bring her in as a journalist. She's a great writer and she's willing to do whatever it takes to get the job done."

"She really did a number on that CEO from California, didn't she?"

"I warned him, he just wouldn't keep his nose out of my business. And don't forget she helped alter the outcome of that New York senate race back in 2000."

"No one will ever forget her reporting on that one."

"Yeah. Eve will take care of those three, I'm sure of it."

"Beyond that, Boss, there are a few people with businesses which I will arrange to have competitors open up right beside them. With our resources, it shouldn't take too long to put most of them out of their misery."

"Good. We can open any kind of business as quick as you need it. Cars, retail, you name it, we can get you up and stocked quickly. Do you need some muscles to get things set up?"

"Yeah. Send me a few beefcakes to do the physical work. Then we'll need several guys who can manage some retail businesses. I'll need a sales manager for a car lot and a real estate broker, too. If I think of some others, I'll shoot you an email in the morning. Better send a truck of office furniture and equipment to get all these people up and running. I'll start renting the spaces this week and should have some of the businesses ready to go by the end of next week."

"Sounds like you have things under control."

"That's right, Boss, but I've got a couple odd ones I'm not sure how to approach. The first stood up and told a story of getting pregnant in high school. This woman was no high school student. She looked to be in her fifties. Said she gave the baby up for adoption. Not much to go on there."

"Yeah, I agree. When Eve gets in town, let her dig around. Not even sure what kind of story she could write at this point to affect her. Might have to let that one go. What's the other one?"

"There is a cop that seems to be hanging around Jenny, the girl who owns the café."

"Did you talk to him?"

"Yeah, he helped play host at a reception that was held at the Bluebird after the memorial service."

"Does he seem connected to the girl?"

"Yeah, I think there might be something there."

"I want him out of the picture right away, top priority," he said vehemently. "I don't need a cop sniffing around there."

"When you say, 'out of the picture,' do you mean permanently, like an accident?"

"No. I don't want to raise any suspicions. I was thinking along the line of a career move."

Robb reached for the map that was lying on his bed. "Um… There is Richmond, which looks to be about two hours away. Then, of course, you have DC, which is about four hours away."

"I was thinking about a place a little smaller, a place where we might be able to influence a sheriff, if you know what I mean?"

"Well, you've got three universities about three or four hours away, James Madison University, University of Virginia, and Virginia Tech."

"A college campus could be very distracting for a young man. I was thinking about something a little closer so we could drag out the heartbreak. You know how difficult it is to keep a long distance relationship alive."

"Well, there is a little town about an hour and a half away that's right on Interstate 95 called Emporia."

"Sounds like a place to check out. Drive out there one day early this week and check it out. Report back to me before you contact the sheriff."

"Boss, I have to say, that I'm not so sure this guy will go out there."

"We may have to sweeten the pot some, but I'm sure we can convince this young man to go. I want to make sure he's out of the picture before too much happens. He might have the smarts to put all this together. As for the rest of those church-goers, I want them squashed like bugs."

"Operation 'flyswatter' is underway."

"Oh, I love that name," the boss responded. "Now don't let that champagne get warm. Make sure you keep focused, and don't let those bikinis get you too distracted from your main purpose there."

"I think I can handle some bikinis and get my job accomplished too," Robb laughed.

"You always seem to. Keep me informed of your progress, and I don't mean with the bikinis." Robb laughed and the line went dead. The boss sat quietly in his dark office. He reviewed the conversation in his mind and smiled. "OK, Charlie," he said out loud, "now that you're in the grave, I'm going to destroy all your good work." He slapped his desk as if he was squashing an ugly bug.

Meanwhile, Robb drained his third glass of champagne and put on his swimsuit. He headed down to the beach where he hoped to find a few young ladies who were looking for a good time. Although Robb didn't possess six pack abs, he was in great physical shape. It took Robb less than an hour to find a couple of young ladies to come up to his room. Several guests turned and stared at the girls in their skimpy bikinis. Robb's smile only grew bigger with each passing glare.

In the room, the Jacuzzi bubbled just like the champagne. Room service brought steaks and more champagne for all three of them. Robb smiled and laughed because he knew he was on his way to a memorable evening and a resounding bug-squashing success.

ABOUT THE AUTHOR

Doug Creamer has been teaching Marketing Education for nearly thirty years. He earned his National Board Certification in 2002 and has helped to develop and write two curriculum guides for the state of North Carolina. He was recently honored with the North Carolina Marketing Education Association's Marketing Education Teacher of the Year. His other books are The Bluebird Café and Revenge at the Bluebird Café. He lives with his wife in Salisbury, North Carolina where he can be found outside working in his yard if he isn't working on his website or writing.

Made in the USA
San Bernardino, CA
24 October 2017